I0105537

Summer Light

Encounters with a Vibrant World

Craig Newberger

Illustrations by Sherrie York
Photographs by Steve Morello
Appendix by Ron Smith

Grackle Publishing - Ambler, Pennsylvania

Grackle

An imprint of Grackle Publishing, LLC

gracklepublishing.com

Copyright © 2023 Craig Newberger

All rights reserved.

Library of Congress Control Number: 2023932332

ISBN: 978-1-951620-19-6

No part of this publication may be reproduced, distributed, or transmitted in any form or by any means, including photocopying, recording, or other electronic or mechanical methods, without the prior written permission of the publisher, except in the case of brief quotations embodied in critical reviews and certain other noncommercial uses permitted by copyright law. For permission requests, write to grackle@ gracklepublishing.com.

In memory of my beloved mother

Gloria Gardner Newberger

Beacon of Light

1928-2022

Summer Light: Encounters with a Vibrant World

Preface

Memories of summer surface often to sustain me through the storms, challenges, and opportunities that each year holds. My mind has wandered repeatedly to a starlit night in August when I was sitting with a group of campers on a rocky ledge overlooking Muscongus Bay on the Maine coast. I was awed by the infinite number of stars twinkling above me and at the same time reflected in the water. For the next hour, we witnessed dozens of celestial sparks streaking across the sky. This was the Perseid meteor shower.

I have known summer days to hold the luscious taste of wild blueberries handpicked on a mountain ridge, the heavenly aroma of sweet pepperbush growing along a shaded stream, the velvety feel of mullein leaves thriving in a field of wildflowers, and the ethereal sound of a hermit thrush echoing through a spruce-fir forest cathedral. These interactions remind me that I am part of a complex world filled with connections and celebrations that thrive on understanding and care.

In these pages, I reflect on the season of summer when light, in a variety of forms, seems ever present. On the longest day, the northern end of the earth's axis tilts directly toward the sun, giving us the summer solstice. Between fourteen and fifteen hours of sunlight reach the temperate regions of our hemisphere at this time. As we move forward through the summer months, the rotation of the earth's axis away from the sun shortens the amount of daily sunlight, signaling changes to come.

Insects make the most of these long summer days. Butterflies coursing through meadows, dragonflies hovering over ponds, and bees nectaring at blossoms are at their busiest. The percussive interludes of grasshoppers and cicadas form the backdrop of the day's activities, yielding to the crickets and katydids during the twilight and evening hours.

Reptiles and amphibians thrive in the warmth of summer. Turtles and snakes bask in sunlight, raising their body temperature and storing warmth. Rainy days encourage salamanders to trade the cover of darkness for a feast of insects, spiders, slugs, and worms. Mixed choruses of frogs sing throughout the day, joined by gray treefrogs at twilight.

Following the frenzy of spring's territorial and mating activity, birds seem to settle in the early weeks of summer. Along the coast, great colonies of terns, herons, egrets, and gulls nest and raise their young. Inland, young songbirds venture from nests to exercise flight muscles and learn feeding strategies. Forests and fields reverberate with birdsong that delights and inspires us. Summer's seasonal finale, migration, crescendos with the departure of those who journey south.

Land mammals in our temperate region do not participate in the great migrations of those in other geographical locations. Their adaptations allow for survival in both cold and warm extremes. During summer's extended hot and dry periods, some mammal species adapt by lowering their metabolic rate and entering a period of dormancy known as estivation. Typical summer days accelerate the activity of our smallest land mammals, the shrews. By contrast, beavers rest during the heat of the day, emerging at twilight. The largest mammals found in this region make the Atlantic Ocean their home. These are the great whales who plow through the ocean brine, filtering fish and plankton through fringed plates of baleen.

Summer's diverse plant life supports the animal activity present in its location. Utilizing the chlorophyll in their cells, plants convert sunlight, water, and carbon dioxide into the energy needed for growth, flowering, and the production of fruit. An additional assist from visiting pollinators makes possible the cycle of seed to flower to fruit to seed once again. Gardens flourish with strawberries in June, raspberries in July, tomatoes in August, and squash in September. And let's not forget, the by-product of this process is oxygen!

As the sun's light sinks below the horizon, lavender skies darken to black. Now is the time for stars and planets to shine. I have always felt an affinity with night. There are sights, sounds, smells and experiences that only these hours can grant. Twinkling fireflies in a tallgrass meadow, wildflower perfume rising on the breeze, owls hooting from perches above take on an otherworldly feel. There is always something new, something not even imagined that I find when I move through the night.

This book is divided into three sections. The first part highlights the days surrounding the summer solstice when the plant kingdom is thriving and everything is lush and vibrant. The second section focuses on the dog days, the hot sultry days of summer, occurring between early July and mid-August. During this period, the sun occupies the same region of the sky as Sirius, the brightest star in Canis Major. The Romans believed that Sirius radiated so much heat that it was responsible for the season's hottest days. The last section focuses on the transitional weeks of summer with its cooling temperatures and shorter hours of daylight.

With a few exceptions, the flora and fauna in this book can be found throughout the northeastern and mid-western portions of the United States and Canada. Each essay begins with an encounter and continues with information I hope you find interesting. While each chapter shines a spotlight on one or two species, it is important to remember that the tapestry of the natural world, the world that sustains our lives, is reliant on multiple threads being woven together. These threads are the vital relationships between plants and their pollinators, predators and their prey, and humans and their responsibility to keep the tapestry intact.

Dancing Lights of Summer

As a child, I was irresistibly drawn outdoors on a warm June evening. Roaming my backyard, I held a glass jar in my left hand and its lid in my right. I was determined to capture as many fireflies as I could. I was hoping that my jar would be the brightest of all time. I wasn't interested in how they were able to flash and spark; I was amazed that it happened at all. There I stood, in my own backyard, holding magic in a jar.

My friends and I spent hours capturing fireflies in jars. We would try reading books using the light of firefly-filled jars and coordinate group jar releases to create explosions of light. Little did we know that those random flashes were romantic coded messages. We had interrupted their highly ritualistic, and visible, courtship displays. Their use of cold light was indeed a unique and effective method for attracting a mate—and young children.

During the day, adult fireflies reside within grasses, wildflowers, shrubs, and trees where they are seldom noticed. Beneath the night sky in open fields covered with dew, they emerge to find their mates. Every detail of the display is performed with utmost precision. The male flies above and blinks his light on and off, while the female hides in the grass and waits for a specific signal. They may exchange flashes several times before the male approaches the female to mate. Once she has accepted his advance and they have successfully mated, she ceases to flash. The male leaves, continuing to shine his beacon, in search of additional females with which to mate.

The number of flashes, the interval between flashes, the color of the light, and the movement of fireflies are all signals that distinguish one species from another. The common eastern firefly, *Photinus pyralis*, produces three flashes in a series. *Photinus brimleyi*, commonly referred to as the sidewinder, produces one long flash. One species is known for its J-shaped flying pattern, while another is known for flying in a straight line. Some fireflies prefer to fly low to the ground and others choose to fly high in the treetops. There are even a few species that synchronize their flashing patterns. Scientists believe that these males flash in unison to help the female locate them. One genus of fireflies, *Photuris*, takes advantage of precision coding in a different way. In addition to emitting her own signal to attract a mate, the female mimics the signals of other firefly species. Unsuspecting males attracted to this female become her prey.

Don't be fooled by the common names: firefly, lightning bug, and glow-worm. These are all used interchangeably. The animal is not a fly, a bug, or a worm. It is a beetle, an insect with stiff armorlike outer wings which hide the soft membranous hind wings used for flying. Beetles represent, by far, the largest order of insects. There are over 350,000 described species of beetles on our planet. The British geneticist and evolutionary biologist, J. B. S. Haldane, who rarely spoke about religion, remarked that "God has an inordinate fondness for stars and beetles." Fireflies represent a special family of beetles, called Lampryidae, which means lantern-bearer.

Like other beetles, fireflies undergo complete metamorphosis moving through the four stages of egg, larva, pupa, and adult. They spend most of their lives as small grublike creatures living underground and feeding on earthworms, snails, and slugs, which they paralyze by injecting them with a numbing chemical. Once they have changed into adults they feed on nectar, pollen, and at times other fireflies. Some adults don't eat at all. The sparkling displays of fireflies are short-lived, seldom lasting more than a month. How lucky we are to witness this dazzling finale to a life mostly hidden from view!

Unlike the warmth generated by incandescent lights, the glow of a firefly is cold. Scientists theorize that billions of years ago oxygen was all but absent in the atmosphere. As oxygen levels rose, the early organisms found it toxic. To survive, some developed bioluminescence to burn off undesired oxygen. Later, when oxygen became an established part of our atmosphere, they retained their oxygen-burning adaptation. Using their bioluminescent ability, fireflies developed a coded courtship display. Other organisms that produce this cold light include algae, fungi, bacteria, one-celled animals, squid, marine worms, and deep-sea fishes. There is nothing as spectacular as swimming or boating under a night sky in water awash with sparkling dinoflagellates, found primarily in marine environments though occasionally found in freshwater. The production of cold light can be attributed to a chemical reaction involving four ingredients in the presence of oxygen: luciferin and luciferase (both named after the Roman god of light, Lucifer), ATP, (a compound that supplies energy for cells), and magnesium. The famous entomologist, Jean Henri Fabré, conducted a series of experiments to see if he could stop a group of captive fireflies from shining their lights. He fired a gun next to their cage, sprinkled water over the insects, and surrounded them with smoke. Nothing stopped the fireflies from flashing on and off.

Numerous legends credit fireflies and other bioluminescent insects with changing the course of history. There is a story told of a doctor in the tropics who performed a critical operation during a power failure using only the light of fireflies. Another tale links the flashes of glowing click beetles, known as headlight elators, to the establishment of a British settlement in Jamaica instead of Cuba where they first landed. It seems that upon their arrival in Cuba, they saw thousands of lights shining in the woods. Suspecting these flickering lights to belong to Spaniards with torches, they retreated to their boats and headed in the direction of Jamaica.

I'll never forget when a friend of mine, visiting from northern California, saw fireflies for the first time. His excitement was off the charts! Dazzled beyond belief as he was surrounded by these little nightlights, he was convinced they were magic. Sadly, over the course of my lifetime, I've watched the magic dwindle. There are far fewer fireflies around today than there were fifty years ago. In fact, one third of the species of fireflies in the United States are endangered. This escalating change is largely due to habitat loss, overuse of pesticides, and the increasing light pollution accompanying buildings and roads. Fortunately, there are many things we can do in our backyards to help bring back the fireflies and their flashes of light.

We can provide a suitable environment for fireflies by growing native gardens, installing water features, and allowing the grass to grow higher in places. We can provide habitat for firefly larvae by keeping leaf litter and woody debris around the margins of our lawns. Turning off our lights at night makes it is easier for fireflies to find mates. Avoiding the use of chemicals and experimenting with natural alternatives to enhance the growth of plants makes yards safer for fireflies and other native pollinators. Finally, we can help monitor the populations of fireflies by participating in a community science project like Firefly Watch. These simple steps can make a world of difference in protecting creatures that have brought so much joy and magic to our lives.

Flash. Tonight's performance has begun. I settle in to watch. This night, I do not have a jar. I do not race to catch light with my hands. Tonight is for watching and savoring. Green lights flicker on and off from the treetops. Yellow lights sparkle in the misty hollows of tall grass. Weaving in and out, dancing to and fro, the night is alive with fireflies.

Expressway Surprise

One morning in June 2021, I woke to dawn skies promising a sun-filled day. On this occasion, I did not wake up early to greet the sunrise or watch the birds. I had an 8:00 a.m. doctor's appointment at the Perlman Center in Philadelphia and I needed to be on time. Aware that rush hour traffic on the Schuylkill Expressway could present a variety of obstacles, my wife and I synchronized our alarm with daybreak. Heading out the door, disappointment settled over me. I would be spending this glorious early morning indoors. It never occurred to me that this morning might hold a memorable discovery.

Traveling south on I-476 we merged onto the Schuylkill Expressway in West Conshohocken. To our surprise, the traffic was moving most of the time, a rare event on the Schuylkill during rush hour. COVID-19 was still in charge of people's daily travels and that meant less traffic as many were still working remotely. Even so, there were enough cars, trucks, and buses on the Schuylkill that morning to slow and often stop traffic. During these slowdowns and stops, my wife and I would glance at the rocky outcrops to our right. In our quest for patience, we spent time checking out the geology and identifying roadside plants. This morning, we were in luck. Miles of highway were bathed in a floral display radiating the early morning sunlight.

From the Conshohocken curve to Girard Avenue, the property on either side of the Schuylkill Expressway was a veritable garden of yellow and white spires. Everywhere we looked, we saw two species in the same genus, common mullein (*Verbascum thapsus*) and moth mullein (*Verbascum blattaria*). Multiple yellow and white blossoms spaced along a tall spire approximately two feet in height, seemed to glow in the morning's sun. Open in the early morning hours, they often wilt and fall to the ground on hot afternoons. The following day, new blossoms appear further up the spire to repeat a brief appearance. Daily, new flowers appear until all the fertilized blossoms have formed small, round compact seed pods. On this morning, miles of blossoms opened creating buttery yellow and white mullein moments in the sun. Stunning.

Plants like common and moth mullein may be disparaged as "weeds," but they are truly pioneers, the first to take advantage of open spaces in the landscape. They thrive in places unsuitable for other members of the floral kingdom. Few environments are as inhospitable for plants as an expressway where they are subject to extreme temperatures, eroded soils and high concentrations of road salt used in winter storms. Still, these sturdy plants thrive in areas hostile to most common garden plants.

Both species of mullein were brought to North America from Europe, Asia, and North Africa, becoming well-established by the 1800s. Highly aggressive, they outcompete our native vegetation and have few requirements for growth. Alongside the Schuylkill Expressway, mullein grows on bare soil or through cracks in the rocks. A single plant can produce over a hundred thousand tiny seeds, which remain viable for years.

Common mullein is known by a variety of names, each one attesting to human uses of the plant. Roman soldiers dipped the long stalks in tallow to make torches, giving it the name, torchwort. Quaker girls, forbidden to use makeup, would rub the hairy leaves on their cheeks agitating the skin cells and producing a red reaction, or contact dermatitis, thus giving it the name, Quaker rouge. Another name, blanket leaf, refers to the soft velvety feel of the leaves, created by the numerous interlocking branched hairs. This feature allows the leaves to conserve moisture while absorbing sunlight and fending off desiccating winds. Additionally, the hairs protect the plant from insects and other animals.

Moth mullein does not have the same type of hairy leaf as the common mullein. Its common name is associated with the purple stamens found in the center of the flower that resemble a moth's feathery antennae. For centuries, it was used as a natural cockroach repellant. In fact, the species name, *blattaria*, is derived from *blatta*, the Latin word for cockroach. Researchers are investigating ways to use moth mullein to control mosquitoes. A methanol extract of the plant killed fifty percent of the mosquito larvae in a simulated pond.

The extraordinary tenacity of this plant was revealed in one of the world's longest running experiments. Back in 1879, an investigation was initiated by botanist, William J. Beal, a correspondent of Charles Darwin, with the goal of finding out how long seeds could survive in the soil. He planted the seeds of twenty-three common plants in twenty narrow-necked bottles filled with moist sand in a secret underground location on the campus of Michigan State, with the plan to dig up one bottle every five years. In his words: "Each vessel was left uncorked and placed with the mouths slanting downwards so the water could not accumulate about the seeds." When he retired, he passed the experiment on to colleagues, who extended the time frame of the experiment, uncovering a bottle every twenty years. When a bottle was unearthed in 2000 and its seeds planted, twenty-one out of twenty-three species of seeds failed to grow. Meanwhile, twenty-three out of fifty moth mullein seeds germinated and grew into successful plants. The only other plant that produced results was round-leafed mallow, sprouting a single seed. Delayed in 2020 due to COVID restrictions, the experiment resumed in April 2021. A week after planting the seeds, two tiny leaf-sprouts popped up from the soil, and eventually eleven moth mullein plants germinated successfully.

Both species of mullein are considered biennials (plants that live for two years). When the seeds sprout in spring or summer, a large rosette of leaves and a taproot form the base of the plant. The rosette of leaves overwinters, and during its second spring or summer, it produces a tall flower stalk and blooms. Occasionally, a flower stalk will wait for its third year to bloom.

Although both species are considered highly invasive, there are many pollinators attracted to their flowers. Halictid bees (sweat bees) and syrphid flies (bee mimics) hover and touch down for a meal of pollen. Bumblebees employ a unique technique called buzz pollination. They grasp the flowers with their mandibles and vibrate the flight muscles inside their thorax, causing the pollen to be released from the anthers of the flowers. This allows them to gather a dusting of orange pollen on their body hairs and rub the pollen onto their legs. Another type of bee, the carder bee, uses the fuzzy hairs on the common mullein leaves as a waterproof lining in its nests.

The gifts of wildflowers are abundant and pleasing to the eye. Southern California has its rolling hills of exquisite orange poppies. Coastal Maine has its eye-popping fields of pink and purple lupines. And, as I have witnessed, Philadelphia, Pennsylvania has stunning rocky outcrops strewn with yellow and white mullein in plain view for all to see on the Schuylkill Expressway.

Summer Snow

On rare occasions, we find ourselves in the right place at the right time. That's where I found myself one afternoon as I stood on a mountaintop, a few days after the summer solstice. It was my second time up this steep slope. Known for its rocky outcrops and challenging terrain, this climb has become a favorite of mine. When I made the trek a year before, in late July, the four-state view was impressive, but on this day, I found it breathtaking. Standing on the summit of this mountain in the Berkshires of western Massachusetts, it looked like miles and miles of forest were cloaked in white. Certainly, this would be the case in the middle of January, but this was a day in June. Through binoculars, it was clear that the land below was resplendent with the blossoms of mountain laurel, a common and, in my estimation, glorious shrub.

Mountain Laurel is a plant belonging to the heath family. The heaths are a staple of the plant kingdom, numbering over four thousand species worldwide. The moors of Great Britain are covered with heather, the most abundant plant in this family. In the United States, there is only one species of wild or native heather, though many of its relatives are found here including bearberry, blueberry, huckleberry, cranberry, rhododendron, azalea, Indian pipe, and laurel. The plants in this family consist largely of small shrubs and vines, preferring regions that are cool, damp, and shaded. Heath balds, frequently found in the southern Appalachian Mountains, are high elevation shrublands, dominated by various evergreen shrubs in this family.

Three members of the laurel genus are widely distributed in the northeast. Sheep laurel, with flowers clustered around the stems,

19

prefers open areas, either dry or wet. Pale laurel, a smaller plant with flowers at its terminal branches, thrives in bogs and other wetlands. The mountain laurel, an understory shrub of the forest, is a larger relative. Its showy flowers, shaped like pentagons, form dense clusters against its evergreen leaves. Able to thrive in places other plants avoid, mountain laurel carpets shaded hillsides, ravines, and rocky slopes. Growing in sizeable stands or thickets in rocky, acidic soil, it spreads aggressively through the production of new shoots at its roots and "layering," which occurs when one of its branches touches the ground and becomes rooted in the soil.

Many are drawn to the natural beauty of mountain laurel. Its delicate white and soft pink flowers resemble a five-sided bowl. Radiating from the center, where its slender pistil stands erect, are ten arching stamen each resting their tiny anthers in small pockets below the flower's edge. Underneath the flower clusters are narrow, oval-shaped evergreen leaves. These lustrous leaves provide contrasting color and structure further highlighting the blossoms delicate splendor. In the past, many became so captivated by its beauty that mountain laurel harvests routinely took place in several localities, generating concern for the plant's survival. In fact, its desirability as a plant for decorative purposes prompted the state of Connecticut to pass a law in 1917 to prohibit stealing the plants from private property for sale.

Scientists have discovered that mountain laurel has one of the fastest mechanisms for pollen dispersal in the floral kingdom. It can shoot its pollen at a top speed of eight miles an hour. Primarily pollinated by native bumblebees, the plant has perfected its form of explosive pollination. When a bee or other pollinator lands on a flower, the stigma, found at the top of the pistil, brushes the pollen from previous flowers off the insect. At the same time, the spring-like stamens, loaded with the flower's own pollen, fling fresh pollen strands onto the bee. Both flower and bee benefit as pollen from neighboring flowers is deposited when new pollen is acquired. Cross-pollination completed.

In fall, the petals die back, revealing capsules containing seeds so tiny they appear as fine brown dust. Each capsule, about the size of a pea, contains over five hundred seeds. When the capsules split open, the seeds are blown aloft by the wind, ready to germinate the following spring.

Although members of the laurel family offer cover for wildlife, their food value to animals, beyond the pollinators who visit, is of little value. Birds, including kinglets and chickadees, have been able to extract benefit from mountain laurel by searching for and feeding on insect eggs lain on the undersides of its leaves. Direct ingestion of leaves, stems, and branches is uncommon as the plant contains two toxins, grayanotoxin and arbutin. These can lead to convulsions, paralysis, and death. Children sucking on the flowers of this plant have experienced poisoning symptoms including burning mouth, vomiting, diarrhea, weakness, and loss of coordination. Even the honey made by bees that visit the mountain laurel should be avoided.

Mountain laurel was first reported in the wild in 1624 by Englishman John Smith in his book *The Generall Historie of Virginia*. Mark Catesby, an English naturalist and artist, describes it in the early 1700s through detailed drawings and etchings of his travels to the Carolinas and Virginia. In 1748, Pehr Kalm, a Swedish botanical associate of Carl Linnaeus, famous for developing modern taxonomy, was sent to the colonies to find new plant species which might also prosper in the Swedish climate. Kalm sent many specimens including foliage from the mountain laurel plant to Linnaeus in Sweden for examination. It was during this same expedition that Kalm noticed some of the sheep accompanying the traveling party had sickened while browsing on mountain laurel leaves. The discovery of mountain laurel's poisonous properties led to one of its common names, "lambskill." Linnaeus recognized Kalm's botanical discoveries by giving mountain laurel the Latin name *Kalmia latifolia*. Once sent across the Atlantic Ocean, mountain laurel became a highly prized ornamental in English gardens. Years later it made its return to North America in the form of several varieties of cultivars.

Like its cousin the rhododendron, the mountain laurel originated in southern climates where unlobed leathery leaves are the norm. Over millions of years, it migrated north to New England. Today, stands of mountain laurel are found as far south as the Florida panhandle and north into the southern regions of Canada. It can be found as far west as Louisiana and Indiana. It is now the state flower of both Connecticut and Pennsylvania. Connecticut designated mountain laurel the status of official state flower in 1907, while Pennsylvania's Governor Gifford Pinchot established mountain laurel as the state flower in 1933 after research proved it to occupy each of the state's sixty-seven counties.

A few places in the United States are known for their outstanding wild mountain laurel displays. These include the Smoky Mountains of Tennessee in late May and the Laurel Highlands of Pennsylvania in early June. A few weeks later, during the final week of June, there is a spectacular display that can be seen if you climb to a mountaintop in the Berkshires of western Massachusetts. Believe me, it's worth being there at the right time and at just the right moment to see this panorama you will never forget—summer snow.

A Little Night Music

It had been an energetic blue-sky day full of discovery and camaraderie. Now, hours after nightfall, I lay comfortably in bed, anticipating a sleep that would replenish my weary yet grateful frame. In the interim, my mind wandered through the events of the day. A group of fifteen inquisitive adult educators had chosen to join me in a hike that would take us around the perimeter of Hog Island on the coast of Maine. Throughout the day, they would experience a variety of habitats from the rocky shoreline to the spruce-fir forest. As I lay waiting for sleep, images of educators scrambling up and over boulders on the shoreline, bending over to inspect tide pools, and shuffling through forests of ferns filled my head. I recalled sounds of laughter, calls of terns and gulls, and the slap of water against the rocks. It was a great day. And then, into my reverie, slipped a very different sound from outside my window—a high-pitched trilling. Gray treefrogs!

One of the most endearing sounds of summer is the voice of the gray treefrog. Not to be ignored, its warbling trill cuts through the stillness of night, traveling a mile or more. Often mistaken for birds or insects, this is the voice of an amphibian seldom seen though frequently heard. It can be quite difficult to isolate the sound though you can bet it is coming from a tree close to a water source. The gray treefrog is famous for seamlessly blending into the environment, making it virtually invisible. When sitting on a branch or the trunk of a tree, a gray treefrog appears chestnut brown or stone gray in color. When surrounded by leaves or lichens, it appears lime or emerald green.

I have found gray treefrogs in some surprising locations—in storm water retention basins adjacent to residential developments, in the trees lining the path of a college campus, and even resting in a flowerpot on the second floor deck of my brother-in-law's townhouse. Their many adaptations allow them to live in a variety of habitats.

Initially, I thought there was only one species of gray treefrog and I was not alone. Genetic research uncovered differences in the chromosomes proving that there are actually two species. Each has a distinct sound or call and preference for geographic location though their populations can overlap. The eastern gray treefrog produces a melodious birdlike trill, whereas the Cope's treefrog emits a faster, higher-pitched sound. The eastern gray treefrogs are more commonly found in the northeast, while the Cope's treefrogs are primarily found in the southern and central states.

Typically about two inches in length, the frogs may be nearly solid in color or they may have beautiful black markings on their back and legs. Most striking is the bright orange-yellow coloration on the inside of their thighs, which they can flash at predators to disorient them. Males and females are almost identical, with the females being slightly larger and the males darker on the undersides of their chins.

Despite its stocky body, the gray treefrog is one of the finest acrobats in the natural world. With legs outstretched, it leaps from limb to limb, defying gravity. It can grab onto a branch with just a few toes and pull itself up until it is comfortably secure. Thanks to the large, rounded pads underneath its toes which contain glands that secrete a sticky mucus, these frogs can attach to and scale all types of vertical surfaces, including glass. These self-cleaning pads both secure the frogs to most surfaces and can clear themselves of any contacted debris. At the Pocono Environmental Education Center in Pennsylvania, I've seen gray treefrogs peacefully resting on a windowpane. Smooth, human constructed surfaces are as easily accessed as plants covered with wet leaves. One could say that they always "stick" the landing.

In fall, gray treefrogs head underground, spending the winter in protected spaces beneath leaf litter, tree roots and stones. About forty percent of their bodies freeze in winter, while their heartbeat and breathing stop completely. They maintain life by producing glycerol, which works much like the antifreeze we put in our cars. Glycerol prevents ice crystals from bursting the cells which would lead to certain death.

On average, gray treefrogs emerge in April, remaining silent for the first week or two above ground. The males start singing when the night temperature is above 50° Fahrenheit and continue for much of the summer. When the male calls, his large balloon-like vocal sac inflates beneath his lower jaw. The sound reverberates substantial distances through the trees and dominates their breeding pools. The tempo increases on warmer nights and slows down as it gets cooler. Each trill lasts approximately half a second with several seconds between trills. On a good night, they might sing for hours. Two other vocalizations are possible to hear if you are in the right place at the right time. The male's courtship call, consisting of a longer trill, occurs when a female is within reach. A second, more aggressive call, made of quick lower frequency vocalizations, is used to ward off other males. Male gray treefrogs are highly territorial and will fight off other males to protect their territories.

The coupling of the male and female in a breeding pool is referred to as amplexus. The male crawls upon the back of a female clutching her with his hind legs. This stimulates the female to release her eggs. She can lay between one to two thousand eggs in small clusters. These eggs are externally fertilized by the male and will hatch in three to seven days, depending on water temperature. Once hatched, it is possible to see a gorgeous orange-vermillion tail with black blotches on the tadpoles. Some believe the tail color to be a form of camouflage called disruptive coloration. This term refers to the breaking up of an animal's outline by a high-contrast pattern of color. Others feel that this coloring warns predators that the skin secretions of the tadpole are toxic.

Following the tadpole stage, lasting a month or two, its two-inch body transforms into a tiny froglet sporting arms, legs, and a tail. The tadpoles remain water bound feeding on algae, aquatic debris, and absorbing nutrients from its tail. Once they transition to the adult stage, they access land more freely, feeding on insects, spiders and occasionally, smaller frogs. Spotting a likely meal, the frog quickly extends its long tongue to capture its prey. Drawing the tongue inside its mouth, the prey is covered in thick saliva. Using its bulging eyes, the frog pushes down on the prey, stimulating the tongue to release it for the frog to swallow.

The sound of gray treefrogs is a wonderful treat on a summer's evening. It is always a delightful surprise when I discover them in a new location. One evening, after playing music for a community dance, our band headed outside to load the instruments and sound equipment into our cars. Although the dance was over, we heard music outside the building. In the distance, sweet melodious trills drifted from the trees. Everyone stopped to listen. The music of the gray treefrogs swept over us as twilight lapsed and stars dusted the sky.

What's the Buzz?

Swat. There are 91,000 described species of insects in the United States, but nothing has attracted as much attention as mosquitoes. Most insects will go about their business without paying attention to the humans that surround them. Mosquitoes will go out of their way to introduce themselves to you.

Swat. We have tried everything … draining, ditching, filling, spraying, and even electrocuting the little rascals. But the mosquitoes are still here. In fact, the implementation of control techniques often destroys the delicate predator-prey balance necessary to keep populations in check.

Swat. I am trying to teach my students about the sanctity of life, swatting mosquitoes as I talk. No matter how many I slap, there are always more. Whether we are outside for a picnic, ballgame, camping trip, or nature walk, the mosquitoes have no trouble finding us.

Worldwide, there are over two thousand species of mosquitoes and most of them would never bite a soul. I remember being terrified as I canoed through a huge swarm of mosquitoes in the Okefenokee Swamp in Georgia. On that occasion, I wasn't bitten once. Of the species that do bite, only the females are equipped with piercing mouthparts. They

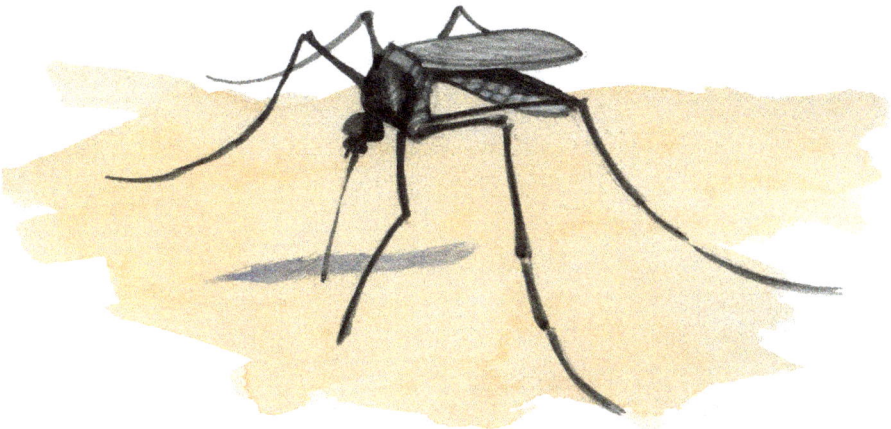

do all the biting and can be merciless. The mouths of males are shaped differently, making it impossible for them to penetrate our skin.

Like many insects, adult mosquitoes receive their energy from the sugar found in nectar. They are irresistibly drawn to flowers and never miss an opportunity to drink the sweet juice. Females require protein, iron and amino acids for the development and ripening of their eggs. The blood of humans and other warm-blooded animals fulfills this need. Without a good blood meal, the female is only capable of laying eight to ten eggs, or perhaps none. With the nutritional supplement that we so kindly provide, she can produce over two hundred eggs at a time.

Mosquitoes use a variety of clues to locate their blood meals. The olfactory receptors in their antennae guide them to detect exhaled carbon dioxide and pick up on our body odor and eventually body heat. Once they land, they taste our skin with their legs to choose the perfect place to bite. Mosquito repellants work by temporarily jamming the pores of the olfactory receptors, making it difficult for the mosquito to detect the chemical stimuli in its environment.

There are no other creatures as perfectly adapted for life with humans as mosquitoes. The proboscis on the female is a marvel of functional design. This long needle-like tube is lined with a series of slender sharp-tipped stylets, used for penetrating the skin. First, the mosquito will moisten its mouth with saliva, lubricating the skin it is about to bite. Then it presses the stylet through the skin into a blood vessel. Once the mouth is firmly in place, the long flexible tube pushes into the opening and draws in the victim's blood. If the victim doesn't bother to swat the mosquito, it will drink for as long as two or three minutes. When the opportunity arises, the female mosquito will take in a load of blood that exceeds her body weight. Despite the extra weight, she can still spread her wings and fly.

The life of an adult mosquito is very short, only a few weeks long in some species. During this brief time, it will mate repeatedly. Hordes of males will fly together, restlessly waiting for a female to pass by. When a female approaches a swarm of males, she is immediately seized by one of the males and through a series of aerial moves, she is fertilized and ready to lay her eggs. Assuming she has recently received a good dose of blood, she seeks out a small stagnant puddle, pool, or pond for egg laying.

Each egg is attached to the next, forming tiny rafts which sit at the top of the water. The eggs hatch in one to three days and become mosquito larvae, often referred to as wrigglers, a term descriptive of their S-shaped swimming pattern. The larvae feed by passing currents of water across their tiny filter hairs. In this way, they absorb vast quantities of microscopic algae, bacteria, and other planktonic substances present in the water. Despite the ruthless reputation of the adults, these water-borne larvae assume the beneficial role of food for larger aquatic organisms.

During their larval stage, they shed their outer covering, or exoskeleton, four times as they grow larger. The next stage of growth requires the mosquito larvae to enclose itself in a pupa. Sometimes called a tumbler, it resembles a round transparent ball with a tail that wiggles just below the surface of the water. While in its pupal stage, it does not feed, though it must breathe oxygen, which it accesses by attaching two tubes called trumpets to the water surface. After two or three days, the curled-up pupa straightens out and splits as the adult emerges to rest on top of the water. Here, it will stretch its body and unfold its wings to dry off in the sun. Once ready to fly, the adult pursues its most important task—finding a mate. Given the exceptionally high mortality rates, there is no time for rest. One population study, focusing on the daily viability of adult mosquitoes, indicates that a third of the population expires every day.

Of course, there is more to life than just finding a mate. While sipping the sweet nectar from their favorite flowers, mosquitoes inadvertently pollinate plants. Most mosquitoes seem to be generalists, pollinating a wide variety of plants; however, there are a few species of orchids that are pollinated exclusively by mosquitoes. I was on a Field Botany excursion in northern Michigan when I first observed this phenomenon. We were examining plants in a quaking bog when we noticed several mosquitoes landing on a rare orchid, the blunt-leafed orchis. My professor was so intrigued by these mosquitoes that he held out his arm, encouraging them to land on it. While he stood there with hordes of mosquitoes biting his arm and hand, he invited us to examine the mosquitoes with our hand lenses. Sure enough, they were carrying globules of bright orange pollen.

It is hard to think positive thoughts about mosquitoes when you are being eaten alive. Still, their importance as both pollinator and prey positions them as vital links in the food chain. At least, we are all treated equally. Fame and fortune aside, everyone is fair game to mosquitoes.

Dragons and Damsels in the Sun

Kayaking on a lake, river, marsh, or swamp excites my explorer spirit. Today's trip takes place on a sizable lake fed by several small streams and thickly bordered by wetland plants, bushes, and trees. Little inlets and coves contour its shores and top my list of places to investigate.

Paddling out into sun-dappled waters, I head across to the nearest cove. My kayak sits low in the water, placing me both below and above it at the same time. Above me, a great blue heron flies, neck tucked tight, expansive wings in motion. Below me, a smallmouth bass swims by. Gliding into the cove, I paddle toward the mouth of a small creek. Pulling close to the shoreline, I spy shiny black whirligig beetles spinning around each other in circles and spirals. Floating on the surface film, their movements are frenzied, and chaotic. Moving on, I decide to check out a jumble of logs and rocks settled in the nearby shallows. As I get closer, I quietly put down my paddle and cautiously pull out my binoculars. Those bumps on the logs turn out to be painted turtles sunning themselves. In my excitement I fail to notice that the current is pushing me closer and closer to them. Suddenly they leap off the log seeking the safety of the water. I am an unwelcome intruder.

Paddling on, I arrive at a bend in the shoreline and see another, larger cove to explore. Up ahead a green heron, partially camouflaged by tall grasses and a leafy thicket of bushes, hunts with halting, carefully placed footfalls. Once spotted, small fish and tadpoles have little chance against the blindingly accurate speed of a heron's beak. Keeping my distance, I steer towards an area full of white water lilies and rusty red water shield. Rooted securely in the muds below, their flat, green leaves float on the surface of the water. Their flowers produce a feast of nectar and pollen for insect visitors. For me, they create a feast for the eyes, reminding me of the artist Claude Monet, who created a series of 250 oil paintings showcasing water lilies.

Here among the fragrant flowers of lilies and water shield, I see them. They are everywhere. Dragonflies and damselflies are going about the business of hunting. They are feeding on the insects that are feeding on the nectar. Bright metallic blue, green and red bodies shimmer past in search of the next meal. A dragonfly lands on the edge of my cockpit. Close up, it is even more intriguing. Careful to remain still, I study its body shape, color pattern, wing length and giant eyes. Dragonflies are fascinating. Moments later, two damselflies land on the blade of my paddle. They lift, hover and land again. I am surrounded by a gathering of multicolored aerialists! Violet dancers, sedge sprites, and elfin skimmers are a few of the common colorful names descriptive of their mystique.

While dragonflies and damselflies share many similarities in physical structure and behavior, there are significant distinguishing features. A dragonfly's body is thicker and more substantial than that of the slender, delicate damselfly. Some say a dragonfly at rest resembles a helicopter with wings held horizontally. A damselfly's body, often smaller in comparison, has a slender, narrow abdomen tendering it a more fragile appearance. At rest they hold their wings pressed together and in an upright position. Both occupy a similar niche in the food chain as predators.

Dragonflies and damselflies are placed in the insect order, Odonata, Greek for "toothed one". The fiercely toothed lower jaws, or mandibles, of the adults are formidable. They hunt for mosquitoes, gnats, mayflies, butterflies, bees, and other flying insects. Once a prey item is chosen, they employ their long hind legs to grab it midair. They take their prey to a perch where they use their powerful serrated mandible to consume it. Often referred to as mosquito hawks, they deserve our thanks for eating huge amounts of mosquitoes, midges and biting flies every day.

Dragonflies and damselflies are among the fastest of all insects, clocking speeds upwards of thirty-five miles an hour in short bursts.

Their gossamer wings, fortified by a network of veins and cells, move independently of one another, making it possible to fly forward, backward, and sideways at will. They are also able to hover motionless in midair when need arises.

While many other insects depend on smell or touch to locate their food, dragonflies and damselflies rely entirely on sight when hunting. The large protruding eyes of these insects, consisting of thousands of six-sided facets, occupy the bulk of their heads, giving them nearly 360-degree vision. All insects have compound eyes, however, those in the order Odonata have more individual lenses per eye.

Ever present on warm, sunny days like this one, I have found them clinging motionless to the undersides of stems and leaves in the presence of clouds or rain. Like all cold-blooded insects, they rely on the sun's rays for warmth and energy. Hours before dawn, they rest in a trancelike position, until the sun's light warms the surrounding air. As the air temperature rises, movement is restored and daily behaviors resume.

Watching the visitors to my boat make quick flights from paddle to stern and cockpit to bow, I reflect on their resemblance to their ancestors from another era. Two hundred forty to three hundred million years ago, before the reign of the dinosaurs, the ancestor of dragonflies, meganisoptera, with a wingspan nearing thirty inches, ruled the sky. Fossilized evidence reveals wing impressions preserved in sedimentary rock, mud, and amber. Modern day dragonflies and damselflies retain many similar features to their ancestor, although they are considerably smaller.

Most of the numerous adults I see today will not survive to feel fall's first frost. In fact, many of them only live for several weeks. As I begin paddling out of the cove, two adults flying in tandem cross in front of me. I have seen this type of coupling many times and know it to be a mated pair. Once the female has been fertilized, the male clasps her neck with the appendages at the end of his abdomen and escorts her to a suitable place to lay her eggs. In some species, the male hovers over the female, keeping her well hidden as she deposits her eggs in the water or upon partially submerged aquatic vegetation.

The female will lay hundreds of eggs, though predators may consume some of the eggs and others might not hatch. Eggs are also vulnerable to physical factors including flooding or a decrease in water level. It is the quantity of eggs lain that ensures the survival of her species. In approximately two weeks, the surviving eggs will hatch to become dun-colored nymphs. The nymphs will spend their next two years living under water. At this time, they bear little resemblance to their air breathing, flying adults. Clad in protective outer skeletons called exoskeletons, the growing nymphs shed their exoskeletons multiple times.

Dragonfly nymphs situate themselves underneath rocks and among the layers of vegetation where they are protected and able to find food. They draw water into their abdomens, running it over their internal gills, extracting life sustaining dissolved oxygen. Dragonflies also use this adaptation to propel themselves forward like tiny torpedoes when potential meals are spotted. As it nears its prey, the nymph shoots out its large lower jaw, or labium, equipped with two sharp hooks at the tip. This hinged labium latches on to the unsuspecting victim, then snaps back into the nymph's mouth. All this happens at breathtaking speed, garnering dragonfly nymphs the title of ferocious predators.

Comparatively, damselfly nymphs are equipped with three feathery appendages resembling tails at the end of their abdomens. These are the gills through which they take in dissolved oxygen. The nymphs maximize the collection of oxygen by waving their gills as they move. Like the dragonfly nymphs, damselflies seek the protective crevices of rocks and bottom debris. They also possess a hinged jaw used to capture and devour prey. When examined closely, tiny wing pads can be seen on the backs of both dragonflies and damselflies behind the head and on top of the thorax or chest. Another shared similarity between them are the two hooks at the end of each segmented leg. Important for the secure attachments they provide, these hooks help the nymphs cling to the underside of rocks when water flows increase.

I've had many remarkable encounters with dragonflies and damselflies. I witnessed a swarm of shadow darners crossing the Delaware River and a large group of green darners travelling south past the north lookout at Hawk Mountain. However, my most notable memory of these mysterious creatures has been the experience of watching an adult dragonfly emerge from its exoskeleton.

Countless times every summer, miraculous natural events take place. I count myself lucky to have witnessed a few of these events in my lifetime. On one occasion, I woke early to a reddish orange blaze of light spanning the horizon. I quickly dressed, found my cap, and headed down to Slough Pond. I arrived at the pond just as the sun breached the trees and scanned the area for wildlife activity. Immediately, I noticed something new at the edge. There was a tuft of tall grasses whose roots were submerged. On one of the blades was a translucent brown exoskeleton. I had seen these many times before on trips to ponds and local waterways. But this time was different—something was moving inside.

Suddenly the exoskeleton split down the middle. A tiny hump appeared, followed soon after by the emergence of a distorted looking creature with crumpled wings. For several minutes, it rested upon the grass stem until minute pulsating movements began sending blood throughout its body. The wings grew larger and its abdomen lengthened. Once dried, the dragonfly was hardened for its first flight. Fully formed, it took to the sky, leaving behind its last shed, or exuvia, the only evidence of time spent as a nymph. I've read many accounts describing the emergence of a dragonfly from its final nymphal exoskeleton to adult. On this day, I saw it myself. What a way to start a day!

A Farewell to Arms and Legs

In the late 1980s, my wife and I rented an old farmhouse on forty-two acres. It was a cold day in December when we traveled down the gravel lane to begin our country life. This small two-story white stucco surrounded by remnant woods and farm fields had plenty of character. Half the house was built in the 1700s and the other half added in the 1800s. Ceilings were floors to the stories above and the basement featured an underground stream. We embraced this woodsy setting for several years to discover that we were not the only ones. Foot thick stone walls hosted numerous additional wildlife tenants.

Every August, shortly before classes started at school, we would find baby eastern milk snakes in the house. One of us would be sweeping or moving a rug and find a small, pencil thin body curled underneath. Startled, it would flee to find refuge in an opening between the floorboards. Though the element of surprise would momentarily interrupt my sweeping, I knew there was nothing to fear. In fact, I looked forward each year to their annual appearance and would bring one for a brief stay in my classroom terrarium. Our houseguests became hands-on, eyes-on ambassadors for the reptile world. They promoted their place in the ecosystem when we discussed habitats and food chains. Once all the classes had opportunities to view and learn about the snake, I took it home and released it in the field behind the house.

We never saw an adult during our cleaning efforts although we speculate that they took advantage of the cracked stone and stucco exterior. These would make easy entrances to enter the walls and lay their eggs. On a few late summer days, we happened upon adult milk snakes sunning in the yard. Frequently found in barns, their name originates from the false belief that these snakes would milk a farmer's cows. This falsehood promoted the idea that milk snakes were pests and should be exterminated upon sight. In actuality, snakes are drawn to barns where they eat the mice and other rodents which are feasting on the grains fed to the livestock, making them beneficial allies for farmers.

At my current house, I see garter snakes on a regular basis in the lawn, sunbathing along the rock wall and curled up inside the compost bin. The snake's common name is derived from the three yellowish stripes on its back, which are said to resemble garters men wore to hold up their socks. Widespread and familiar snakes, they can be found in a variety of habitats including forests, fields, wetlands, and suburban lawns. During mating season in early spring, it's possible to witness a large group moving together or intertwined in a twisting mass with a single female surrounded by many males. Once mated, the female can store sperm in her body until she locates optimal habitat for giving birth. Following a two-to-three-month gestation period, she will bear several dozen live young. Once the young are born, she will move away, leaving them to fend for themselves.

Back in the Cretaceous period, when dinosaurs roamed the earth, snakes moved about on well-developed legs. Over time, they took a unique evolutionary pathway and gave up their limbs. A few species of snakes, including boa constrictors and pythons, have vestigial hind limbs. Some have external spurs and others have bony projections that are only detectable with an X-ray.

Myths, stories, legends, and fables led many to fear the appearance of a snake's forked tongue. Some of these would have us believe that the forked tongue of a snake is sharp or poisonous. In truth, snakes use their tongues to pick up chemicals present in the air. Flicking their tongues in and out, snakes capture scent molecules. They pass these over the Jacobson's organ located in the roof of their mouths. Here, the information gathered by the tongue is translated and relayed to the brain, assisting the snake in assessing its immediate surroundings, including scents left by other snakes and potential prey.

Technically, there is no such thing as a poisonous snake. Poison is something that one ingests. Venomous snakes produce venom for defense and assistance in the digestion of prey. It is injected through the snake's hollow fangs into the flesh of an animal. Less than twenty percent of snake species in the world are venomous and most of these are found in the tropics. Two hundred species of venomous snakes are medically important. Snake venom is used for chemotherapy and its toxins have applications for treating strokes, heart attacks, and pulmonary embolisms. Only three venomous snake species, the timber rattlesnake, the eastern massasauga, and the copperhead are found in the mid-Atlantic and northeast regions of the United States, and they are listed as threatened or endangered by state wildlife agencies.

The northern watersnake, a fully aquatic snake, is a common inhabitant in ponds and streams. During frequent visits to the Wissahickon Creek, my students have been able to observe watersnakes swimming and basking on rocks at the water's edge. The color pattern on the adults may include black, brown, or varying shades of gray, while the juveniles are more brightly colored. Found throughout the eastern United States, watersnakes feed on fish and amphibians. Like garter snakes, the young are born alive.

My favorite is the hognose snake, which I have found in the coastal sand plains of Cape Cod and the New Jersey Pine Barrens. Although its color and pattern are variable, it blends seamlessly with its environment. Its upturned snout does the work of a trowel as it sweeps side to side, digging in the sand. A consummate performer, this snake is known for its intriguing defensive behavior. When approached, it will inflate its body, hiss loudly, and flatten its neck. Then it will raise its head above the ground like a cobra, giving it the surname "puff adder." On occasions, it will open its mouth as if to strike, but it won't bite. At the completion of this routine, the snake rolls over on its back and plays dead like an opossum, complete with its mouth wide open and tongue sticking out. When I worked for the Cape Cod Museum of Natural History, I took groups to a private junkyard where there were heaps of old boards scattered around. Breaking into small groups, the students picked different areas of the junkyard to explore. Each one was eager to be the first to find a hognose snake underneath a broken board.

Eventually someone's high-pitched shout would send everyone running to get a good look.

The largest snake in our area, the black rat snake, is typically four to six feet long, though some can grow to nine feet. An excellent climber, it stretches and contracts its muscular body as it works its way up a tree. During visits to the Pocono Environmental Education Center, my students and I would follow our guide to inspect a series of large concrete boxes behind a group of old cabins. Black rat snakes were known to enter the boxes and lay beneath the pipes and insulation. Our guide would carefully reach into a box, locate a snake, and lift it up to show the group. He held it so that it could move freely in his hands without fear. In turn the students were able to feel the smooth, dry scales as they learned about its needs for survival. As a constrictor, rat snakes feed by catching, wrapping, and then squeezing their bodies around warm-blooded prey, including mice, chipmunks, and birds.

The only venomous snake that I've encountered in the wild is the northern copperhead. Recognizable by the hourglass shaped pattern on its body and the orangey copper color of its head, this snake is not aggressive. Copperheads prefer secluded rocky hillsides, far from interactions with people. These snakes have heat sensory pits located between the eyes and nostrils which enable the copperhead and other pit vipers to detect tiny changes in temperature. This ability to gauge temperature is key to their success in finding food. Warm-blooded animals that wander within range of their sensors are swiftly detected, becoming the day's meal.

Equipped with unique adaptations for survival, snakes move through the world both as predator and prey. Just as field mice, grasshoppers, and lizards are prey for them, snakes are prey to other species including hawks, owls, herons, weasels, foxes, and coyotes. This summer, a juvenile red-shouldered hawk routinely hunted my yard for snakes. The first time I saw him in possession of his prey I had to chuckle. He seemed confused about what to do with it. Snake dangling from his talons, he flew to the closest tree where he pecked at it from time to time, shifting his feet, looking up at the sky, and flapping his wings. He flew from tree to tree for about twenty minutes performing the same actions each time until he finally settled to feed. Days later, a bony snake carcass dangled from a tree limb.

Snakes are beneficial to us in many ways. According to the Illinois Department of Natural Resources, a medium-sized black rat snake can eat up to nine pounds of rodents every year. A lot of these rodents are the mice that slip into our homes, chewing through bags of dog food and birdseed, then moving on to find their way to the kitchen. Many snakes also keep insect populations in check, assisting us in growing healthy fruits, vegetables, and flowers. Consider yourself lucky if you find a snake in your garden.

Although some people fear snakes, I have found young children to be fascinated by them. They are captivated by their long sleek bodies, lidless eyes, and flicking tongues. Primary students enjoy lying on the ground, arms pinned to their sides, imitating the muscular movements of a snake. When given the chance to examine a snake shed or even better to watch a snake shed its skin, wonder fills the air. Teachers will tell you that they treasure these teachable moments. It is my hope to walk through the world with snakes as interpreters and guides. There is certainly reason to give any wild animal space when encountered. Like us, they will do what they can to protect themselves when threatened. I caution that respectful observation allows both snake and human to move through the world more harmoniously.

There are approximately a hundred and fifteen species of snakes in North America, although I can count the number of species that I've seen with my hands and toes. I have hundreds of species of birds on my bird list, but only fifteen species of snakes on my snake list. Quiet and elusive, snakes do not advertise their presence, moving silently about their daily lives. I feel fortunate to have had several significant encounters.

It seems that no one is neutral when it comes to snakes. It is the same way with olives. My wife loves olives. I do not. My wonderful wife and I find common ground on almost every other issue. When it comes to olives, we agree to disagree. When it comes to snakes, we agree that they are enchanting and wondrous creatures.

Blossoms of the Night

"And 'tis my faith that every flower enjoys the air it breathes."
–William Wordsworth

Many of us travel the world to see natural wonders we've read about in books or seen on a screen. Leaving places we know well to immerse ourselves in those we don't can yield breathtaking moments. Mindful of the powerful impact of personal connection, I arranged trips for students and families to experience the natural wonders of Costa Rica, Iceland, and Alaska. Each trip produced the same result. Participants returned refueled in spirit and energized to make new discoveries. Travel does that for us. It gives us a chance to better understand the rhythms of this world.

Still, there are a host of natural wonders requiring little to no travel. Hiking down a trail, paddling along a stream, or ambling the path in my local park continually yields a bounty of interesting natural treasures. In a vacant lot on a small-town street corner, I witnessed a stunning event I will never forget.

One warm summer's evening, I was invited to a friend's house for dinner. After the meal, we decided to go for an early evening walk in the neighborhood. Stepping outside, I noticed a group of people had gathered down the street and were standing at the corner. They were chatting with each other amicably while gathered around something I couldn't quite make out. However, I was able to see a tiny assemblage of colorful wildflowers among the tall grasses. When I asked my friend what he thought was going on, his answer surprised me. Apparently, night after night his neighbors gathered in this location to watch the flowering of pink evening primroses. Knowing that I had a passion for plants, he guided me toward the group so that we could take in the event. Always up for learning something new, I eagerly followed him.

At 8:45 p.m. on this mild July night, the sun had just finished setting. All eyes were focused on a small patch of primroses. Suddenly, the green sepals surrounding the closed-up flower began to split in four distinct places and the buds began to open. First one sepal fell backwards and then another, and almost instantly the flower unfurled its four pink petals. It all happened so quickly. It was like watching a film clip of time-lapse photography. And then, out of nowhere, there appeared the largest gathering of sphinx moths I had ever seen. Resembling hummingbirds in flight, these moths were on a mission. Somehow, they knew exactly when and where the primroses were going to bloom, and night after night, they returned to feast on nectar. Wings a blur at forty-one cycles per second, they gracefully maneuvered their stout bodies to hover briefly over each flower, feeding on its sugary liquid. Watching this interaction between plant and insect left me speechless. Night-blooming flowers now topped my list of natural phenomena to investigate.

Since that night, I have discovered that many flowers are attuned to evening's low light conditions. Given the interdependence of plants and insects, this makes perfect sense. We, as a species most active and visually aware during the day, assume the same to be true of most animal life. We are used to seeing flowers bloom during the daylight hours and remain open until pollination occurs and seeds are formed. However, the natural world hums, buzzes, clicks, and blooms in tune with summer's shorter, warmer nights. Nocturnal insects need these late day bloomers as nectar and host plants, while the plants need the insects for pollination. Uninterrupted, it is a sustainable strategy for both populations.

Most moths are active at night and seek out white or pale-colored flowers on which to feed. Their long feathery antennae act as chemical receptors seeking the sweet-smelling scent of night blooming flowers. Once located, some moths will hover while others will land on the blossom. Extending its long tube-like proboscis, the moth briefly probes the middle of each flower to take in energy-rich nectar. There are local species of moths with proboscides up to three inches long. In the tropics, there is a species whose proboscis measures ten inches, allowing it access to nectar hidden in the bottom of long tubular blooms.

The stout-bodied caterpillar, or larva, of a sphinx moth has been said to resemble the sphinx of ancient Egypt. Balancing on the stem of a plant or a leaf with its foreparts raised and head curled, it assumes a regal pose. The adult moths, unlike most butterflies, are colored a somber gray or earth-tone brown. They have no need for attractive coloration as they are creatures of the night when shades and shadows prevail. Blending in with the night environs assists their survival, protecting them from predators. Even the antireflective coating on their eyes makes them harder to detect. This coating is so effective in preventing reflected light that it served as an inspiration for Dr. Shin-Tson Wu, a professor of optics and photonics at the University of Central Florida. He worked with a team of scientists to develop a coating for cell phones that would cut down screen glare. Prior to this research, moth eye biomimicry had also been used to enhance the efficiency of solar cells.

Another night bloomer, jimsonweed, features fragrant white to light lavender trumpet-shaped flowers. The blossoms can be hard to detect as they lay hidden beneath the leaves, opening only on late summer and early fall nights. Its "thorn apple" nickname refers to the appearance of its large spiny seed capsules which contain several dozen highly toxic black seeds. A variety of nocturnal moths pollinate these flowers including the large Carolina sphinx moth, whose caterpillar has quite a ravenous reputation. It is commonly known as the tobacco hornworm, aptly named for the "horn" on its last segment. This lime green caterpillar sports thin white stripes spaced at an angle and in a parallel pattern on each side of its body. It is the perfect camouflage for hiding among leaves and vines. Preferred food sources for both caterpillar and moth are those of the nightshade family including jimsonweed, tobacco, and tomato plants. The origin of jimsonweed has confused botanists throughout the centuries. Some cite Asia while others feel it is Central American in origin. We do know that the seeds of this plant have followed humans around the world and jimsonweed is now considered a naturalized plant in North America. Another common name, Jamestown weed, refers to an incident that took place in Jamestown, Virginia. During Bacon's Rebellion of 1676, a group of British soldiers unwittingly ingested its leaves and suffered hallucinations for days. Jimsonweed is considered a poisonous plant and routed out in pastures where it might be eaten by livestock. However, chemicals present in jimsonweed are also important components of medicines used to treat asthma, influenza, and nerve diseases.

It has been a long time since my walk with the primroses and moths. Although I have travelled many places in the world, I am frequently reminded that you don't need to travel far to find natural treasures. Day and night, and the twilight hours in between, wondrous events are taking place all around us.

Ghosts of the Forest

Beginning in late spring, throughout the summer and into early fall, I relish the opportunity to head outside and explore some of my favorite fields and wetlands. Grabbing sunglasses and a wildflower guide, I head out to see what's blooming and what's gone to seed. When I see perennials that return year after year to the same spot, it feels like meeting up with old friends. Each time I see them, I get to know more about them. The next best thing to running into a familiar flower, leaflet, or seedpod is finding something I have never seen before. A fan of brainteasers and mysteries, I am always ready to research a new "resident" in the area.

Things are a bit different when I head into the woods. Forests, with leafy canopies and earthen floors, offer conditions best suited to plants with low-light requirements such as the ferns and mosses. Summer's sun-loving wildflowers cannot tolerate the shade and shadow, moisture, and organic debris of forest habitats. Wildflowers that grow beneath trees and bushes tend to bloom in early spring when sunlight reaches through bare branches to touch the forest floor. Once the trees leaf out, light penetration diminishes. Still, there are a few flowers that have found a way to thrive in the summer's shade-darkened forest and Indian pipe is one of them.

I'll never forget the first time I noticed Indian pipe. I was walking with a friend through our college nature preserve. We were engaged in conversation and paying minimal attention to our surroundings when we suddenly stopped in our tracks. Bending down to examine this strange looking organism, we were mystified. When I returned to my dorm room, I looked it up in my field guide to mushrooms, but none of them resembled what we had seen. It finally occurred to me a few days later to check for it in my Peterson wildflower guide. There it was, on page twenty, under the caption "Small Fleshy Plants, Specialized Habits."

Enchanting and beguiling, the radiant white color lends an otherworldly appearance to Indian pipe. Even its tiny scale-shaped leaves are waxy white. The common name, Indian pipe, describes its resemblance to ceremonial pipes used by North America's indigenous people. Other names based on appearance include "corpse plant" and "ghost plant." The plant's Latin name, *Monotropa uniflora*, aptly describes its appearance. The genus name, *Monotropa,* means single turn, referring to the way its bloom stands erect when pollinated by bumblebees or other insect visitors. The species name, *uniflora*, refers to its single flower which is divided into several parts and measures three-quarters of an inch long at the top of its stem. Following fertilization, a five-sided seed capsule forms. Once desiccated, the capsule releases dust-like, wind-blown seeds through narrow openings running from the top to the bottom of the fruiting body. On a winter's walk through the forest, it's possible to find its blackened dried stems and seed capsules.

Indian pipes are often mistaken for some type of fungi. Its white color, similar to that of many mushrooms, and its preferred location for growth can promote confusion. It can also be puzzling to consider the absence of chlorophyll, normally found in the cells of a flower's stem and leaves. Chlorophyll along with sunlight, carbon dioxide, and water are necessary ingredients for photosynthesis. It is the process of photosynthesis that results in the production of the chemical energy needed for plant growth. Lacking chlorophyll, Indian pipes developed another way to capture nutrients and energy needed for growth. Their strategy involves parasitizing a family of fungi often associated with beech trees.

The fungi attach themselves to the roots of trees, enabling the trees to increase their access to water and nutrients from the soil. The fungal thread-like filaments form an underground network as they move through the soil attaching to the roots of neighboring trees. This fragile web allows for a mutually beneficial relationship between a specialized group of fungi, called mycorrhiza, and the trees in the forest. Messages about a tree's health and insect invasion pass along these mycorrhizal threads. If a tree is compromised by disease or physical damage, additional nutrients can be channeled from other trees to provide support.

Above ground, trees produce sugar through the process of photosynthesis. In turn, the fungi acquire the sugars they need by feeding on the tree's energy-rich sap. Indian pipe takes advantage of this symbiotic relationship and jumps into the middle, taking its energy from the trees via the fungal intermediary. To see how this works, botanists devised a method to trace the passage of sugars from the tree's roots to the mycorrhizal fungi and into the parasitic Indian pipe plants. Radioactive isotopes were injected into the sapwood of trees and found to travel through the roots to the fungi and on to the Indian pipes. A true parasite, Indian pipes take from the fungal threads, giving nothing in return.

The renowned poet Emily Dickinson was captivated as a child by the ghostly Indian pipe and called it "the preferred flower of life." As she grew older and her fascination with the plant increased, she remarked, "Maturity only enhances the mystery, never decreases it." In the first published edition of her poetry, her editor, Mabel Loomis Todd, chose a drawing of the Indian pipe for the cover of the book. Many years later, Mabel's daughter, Millicent Todd Bingham, chose a sketch of the Indian pipe for her mother's gravestone.

Indian pipe is a member of the heath family, a family of mostly shrubs and vines including blueberries, cranberries, azaleas, laurels, and rhododendrons. Within that family, there resides a small subfamily of parasitic species found throughout temperate regions of North America. Pinesap, also known as Dutchman's pipe, is another species that relies on the unique relationship between  mycorrhizal fungi and trees. Less common than Indian pipe, it grows in the acid soils of oak and pine forests. The nodding vase-like flowers cluster at the tip of each fuzzy stem and come in a variety of colors, including white, yellow, pink, red, and purple. In most cases, it is yellow in summer and red in the fall.

If you encounter Indian pipe or pinesap flowers in the forest, it is best to leave them undisturbed. There is no advantage to picking these plants because they will immediately wither and turn black. It is not possible to successfully transplant them to your yard because they depend on the forest ecosystem. They will not survive without the host trees and the fungal intermediaries. Slow to establish from seed, Indian pipe thrives in deep unbroken forests with abundant shade. They are considered good indicators of a healthy ecosystem.

Nature doesn't always operate by the broad generalizations we learned in school. Indian pipe and pinesap have a distinctive method for getting their energy and making use of the soil's resources. They are enchanting plants that challenge our preconceptions and remind us of the rich connections between the various components of the forest community.

Fiddler on the Marsh

Hidden behind the sand dunes lies a fertile place between water and land. This is the world of the salt marsh, where freshwater streams, weaving through woodlands and fields, join ocean waters in tidal creeks. They wind their way through heavy mats of cordgrass and salt meadow hay, covering rich brown muds lain down over time. It is a place of wind and light. Trees have no harbor here where salt and water hold dominion. Fragments of shells and bones left by high tides are scattered throughout the grasses. A torn kelp frond, a skate egg case, and the long brown telson of a horseshoe crab peek through layers of silt. Multicolored buoys, broken styrofoam floats, and weather worn planks speak to the strength of storms long past.

When I worked as a naturalist at the Cape Cod Museum of Natural History, I would frequently take visitors on walks around the periphery of the saltmarsh behind the museum. Not far down the narrow path, we would run into a curious throng of small critters, no larger than two inches across, walking sideways through the marsh grass. As we approached, movement ceased. Suddenly, all together, they made a hasty retreat into tiny holes in the mud. My visitors were at once surprised and mystified. How could such a small creature have such an enormous claw? Eager to get a closer look, we continued down the damp earthen path in hopes of finding another gathering of sideways walkers. It wasn't long before we found several other groups skittering about on the edge of the marsh, along the banks of creeks and down in the mosquito ditches. With each new sighting, everyone stood as still and quiet as possible, poised to get a better look. Sure enough, we were rewarded with several opportunities to observe their movements and interactions with each other.

The plants and animals that live in the salt marsh must be equipped with adaptations to cope with fluctuating salinity, wind speed, and temperature. They must also constantly adjust to the ever-changing tides governed by the rotation of the earth and the pull of the moon. The fiddler crab is well adapted to the half-dry half-wet world of the salt marsh. Like other crabs, the fiddler has gills for swimming in the water. It also has a primitive lung, enabling it to live above and below ground for several days. At times, fiddlers appear as if they are foaming at the mouth. Blowing bubbles is a sign that a crab is transitioning from using its gills in the water to using its lungs to breathe.

The life of a fiddler crab is intertwined with the cycling of the tides. At low tide, hordes of fiddler crabs scurry across the marsh, rummaging through newly stirred debris for fresh food items. As high tide fills the marsh, they make a timely retreat into the refuge of their burrows.

Fiddler crabs dig burrows using their four pairs of walking legs. They pack small particles into pellets, removing them from the tunnels and placing them near the entrance. The burrows can extend approximately three feet down into the mud, sand, or peat, usually ending in a horizontal room. During each flood tide and throughout the colder seasons, the fiddler plugs its burrow entrance with excavated pellets, allowing it to spend extended periods of time in its oxygenated burrow.

The trademark of the fiddler crab is the extra-large claw found only on the male. When the claw is waved back and forth, it resembles someone bowing the violin, thus earning the crab its name. The oversized claw can account for half his body weight and is brightly colored. Used primarily for display, the male waves his claw during mating season to attract a mate. At other times, the big claw is used offensively to ward off other males and defend territory. Male fiddler crabs climb out of their burrows claw first. Conversely, they back into their burrows, flaunting the large claw until well hidden. Tucked away, secure, and armed, the male fiddler is well positioned to guard his compact territory. Remarkably, should the larger claw be lost in battle, his smaller claw will assume the size of his bigger claw. The lost claw regenerates to the size of the smaller one. Close observation of any fiddler crab colony reveals a good mix of right-clawed and left-clawed crabs.

Sporting two small claws, the female crab is more evenly proportioned. These smaller claws make it easier for her to sift through debris and mud for food items. The males depend solely on their smaller claw when eating. A fiddler crab moves pieces of marsh peat to its mouth, where it sorts the peat for edible materials. Inedible matter is sifted out by the mouth parts and formed into tiny spheres of mud and sand which are left along the banks.

If a predator seizes a fiddler crab by one of its legs, the crab will automatically surrender the leg. This self-amputation reflex enables the crab to escape quickly, losing a leg to save its life. During the crab's next molt, the leg will grow back. Often the creeks are littered with battle-worn cast offs comprised of old claws and legs lost in combat.

Mating takes place approximately every couple of weeks during the summer. Females will wander around the colony looking for a viable mate. Males that are larger and have bigger claws are more attractive to the females. They will have larger burrows and are healthier than smaller, younger crabs. Using a robotic claw, Dr. Sophie Mowles of Anglia Ruskin University in Cambridge, England, determined that female fiddler crabs prefer the males with the fastest moving claws.

The male will stand near his burrow entrance, rapidly waving his large claw up and down. An attracted female will stare at him for a short period. The male will skitter back and forth, to and from his burrow entrance. He repeats this until the female accepts him or she wanders off. If interested, the female will approach and tickle him with her legs, signaling that she wants to mate and not steal his home. Once she enters his burrow, he will follow, plugging the entrance behind them. Here, following mating, the female will incubate her eggs for approximately two weeks in a space underneath her abdomen. At the approach of hatching time, she leaves the burrow to transport her eggs to the water's edge, releasing them with several forward thrusts of her abdomen. The eggs hatch in the water to become tiny young fiddler crabs.

As part of the free-drifting plankton community, the young's dispersal and movements are completely at the mercy of the currents. Microscopic in size, they are vulnerable to a wide variety of predators. Each zoea, or fiddler crab larva, is no bigger than a grain of sand, though fully equipped with a head, abdomen, and four pairs of legs.

After several molts, the older larvae are known as megalops (meaning big-eyed). Upon reaching their final larval stage, they molt to become immature crabs and return to land. At this time, males and females look alike. It is as they grow older that the male develops his larger claw.

Fiddler crabs seem to be governed by internal biological clocks, perfectly attuned to their natural habitat. Interestingly, fiddlers have pigments in their shells which expand and contract. At night, the crabs become several shades lighter than they are during daylight. No one is sure whether these color changes serve to camouflage the crabs, protect them from the sun's ultraviolet radiation, or regulate their body temperatures. In an effort to better understand how their biological clocks work, scientists from Woods Hole, Massachusetts collected fiddler crabs from Buzzards Bay, placed them in wooden crates and then shipped them to Berkeley, California. Despite the time difference, the crabs continued to change colors according to Eastern Standard Time.

Fiddler crabs play a significant role in the health of a saltmarsh, contributing to both primary production and decomposition. Their burrows aerate the soil and turn over nutrients, enhancing the growth of grasses, sedges, and rushes. They are a food source for herons, egrets, terns, fish, and waterfowl. And they are fascinating to watch. An assemblage of fiddlers scuttling across a marsh, should not be missed. They are some of nature's most active and engaging residents.

Our Largest Salamander

On April 23, 2019, the governor of Pennsylvania signed into law a resolution designating the eastern hellbender, a large aquatic salamander, as Pennsylvania's state amphibian. Wearing a blue "Hellbender Defender" T-shirt, Governor Wolf declared, "Clean water is critical for the hellbender, and we need to continue to do our part to improve water quality in the commonwealth so that the state's first amphibian can thrive." It had taken years of research and advocacy by a host of volunteers, scientists, and the Chesapeake Bay Foundation's Student Leadership Council to secure this designation. Fans of the eastern hellbender joyously celebrated the near unanimous consent by both parties to add the eastern hellbender to Pennsylvania's list of state species. Meanwhile, the salamanders, true to form, spent their big day out of the limelight, hidden beneath algae covered rocks.

Although superficially resembling lizards, most species of salamanders have smooth moist skin which absorbs dissolved oxygen in the water. Lizard skin is dry, scaly, and comparable to protective armor. Also, lizards have claws on their feet while salamanders do not. Like other amphibians, most salamanders are born in water, eventually spending most of their lives on land. There are exceptions to this rule, such as the hellbender, which is strictly aquatic throughout its life.

Salamanders range in size from the Mexican minute salamander, measuring less than an inch from head to tail, to the giant Chinese salamander, which can grow up to four feet long and weigh as much as one hundred pounds. The eastern hellbender is the third largest salamander in the world and the largest salamander in the western hemisphere. It can grow up to thirty inches long, although on average they measure between twelve and fifteen inches. Adults weigh between four and six pounds.

Legend has it that fishermen named them hellbenders because they look "like they crawled out of hell and are bent on going back." There are also colloquial names alluding to some of its unique physical features. "Old lasagna sides" refers to the frilly undulating skin along both sides of its body resembling wet lasagna noodles. Hellbenders have also been called "snot otters" due to its slippery mucus covered skin. This covering provides protection from scrapes and parasites and is also thought to possess antibiotic properties. Colored a blotchy mud to red brown above with a pale underside, hellbenders are well camouflaged in their stream environment. Spending most of their time beneath large rocks during the day, these salamanders emerge from their dens to hunt for crayfish, fish, and other amphibians at night.

Over the years, I've taken students to one of my favorite places to find reptiles and amphibians in the Pocono Mountains. Each visit included a day spent with a local naturalist whose excitement and enthusiasm for reptiles and amphibians was contagious. We spent our day exploring forests, ponds, streams, and wetlands, looking under rocks, logs, and other debris. Typically, we found over twenty species, including eight or nine species of salamanders. Our naturalist taught the students how to find, handle, and replace the individuals respectfully. He would patiently field question after question as we moved through the forested habitat that was their home. Equipped with twenty pairs of eyes and abundant determination, we found some impressively large species. The spotted salamander and the spring salamander, both measured close to eight inches long though neither could compare to the size of a hellbender. I shared with him my hope to see a hellbender one day. Much to my surprise, he offered to take me to a location frequented by a population of hellbenders. I jumped at the opportunity.

We decided to meet in Jersey Shore, a surprising name for a borough in Lycoming County, Pennsylvania, in the heart of the Susquehanna watershed. The key to finding hellbenders is to locate habitat that perfectly fits their needs. Hellbenders require swift flowing, highly oxygenated, cold water (between 48 and 73 degrees Fahrenheit) and a rocky, not muddy, streambed with lots of large flat rocks jumbled throughout. On both sides of the stream bank, there should be a riparian buffer supporting a variety of vegetation, especially large trees, providing shade and nutrients for aquatic organisms. Together we traveled to a tributary which empties into the Susquehanna River. Our hopes were high that this was the perfect spot to begin our search.

Although many people fish, boat, and swim in these waters, surprisingly few ever see a hellbender. Most likely, that is because these salamanders are active at night, unless it is a late summer's day and they are out looking for mates. My friend set some strict guidelines for our exploration in the creek. He explained that hellbenders are site specific, which means they rarely travel far from a chosen rock. We would need to carefully lift some rocks to be able to find one. After lifting a rock, it was important to put it back exactly the way it was found before moving on to another. If we were lucky enough to locate and handle a hellbender, it was critical that we return it, placing the hellbender in its original shelter.

I located a large flat rock, lifted it, and reached underneath. No luck. I tried again with a different rock, and there was nothing there. The third rock was the charm. I lifted it part way, reached way underneath, and felt a large slimy creature. To be honest, I was a bit scarred. The hellbender is a formidable creature. It has lots of tiny teeth, although it is not known to bite unless scarred. I was careful to be as gentle and nonthreatening as possible. Although nonvenomous, it can exude a foul-smelling musk through its skin when threatened. This was a price I was willing to pay for a transformative encounter with an animal whose appearance on this planet dates back 160 million years. I cradled the hellbender in my wet T-shirt and thought about its Jurassic ancestors. It is said that beauty is in the eyes of the beholder, and in that precious moment, I found this mucus-covered creature to be truly breathtaking. Shortly afterwards, I located two more hellbenders nearby. Thrilled to have seen and held a few of these fascinating creatures, I decided not to disturb any others.

Our excursion took place in the middle of July. We had chosen to steer clear of mating season which begins in August and runs into September. At that time, males entice females to join them under their nest rocks. The females lay a double strand containing one to five hundred eggs, and the males fertilize them externally. Though most reptiles and amphibians abandon their eggs, the male hellbender spends approximately two months guarding them until they hatch. He will stay with them during their larval stage, occasionally eating some of his offspring.

When first hatched, the larvae are about an inch long with external gills branching from their necks. Their diet consists of aquatic insects, including mayfly nymphs and caddisfly larvae. By the age of two, they lose these gills and acquire dissolved oxygen in the water through their skin. They reach sexual maturity around the age of six, and it is estimated that they could live fifty years or more in the wild.

Factors that limit their longevity include pollution, habitat loss, and sedimentation. Hellbenders spend their entire lives submerged in water. Waterways can only remain cool when shaded by trees. Warmer waters hold less dissolved oxygen, falling short of that required by hellbenders. A stream suffering an oil spill or the disposal of organic or chemical pollutants, can devastate hellbender populations. In addition to oxygen, their skin can absorb other substances that make their way into the water without discrimination. Unrestricted development and erosion along our waterways create plumes of mud and silt, filling up the crevices in the large slab rocks that hellbenders need for shelter, mating, and raising young.

Choosing the hellbender as its state amphibian logically signals that the citizens of Pennsylvania understand the importance of protecting the water quality in freshwater streams where they are found. Pollution intolerant, these unique amphibians require fast-flowing, oxygen rich streams flanked by forests which moderate water temperature and shed organic material. Stream bottoms filled with layers of large rocks provide hideaways for both the hellbender and its prey. Should stream conditions be allowed to deteriorate, the hellbender's survival is threatened. Comparable to the canaries once used to detect the potential for disaster in a coal mine, eastern hellbenders can be counted on as reliable indicators of stream health. These sensitive salamanders remind us that land and waterways are connected, each depending on the health of the other. Let us hope that Pennsylvania honors its call to truly be "hellbender defenders."

Flutes in the Forest

Whenever possible, I sleep with the windows cracked open. Hearing the dawn chorus of birds coaxes me to greet the sunrise and join their waking world. I am forever drawn to the vocalizations of birds. Whether I recognize the vocalist or not, the warbles, trills, calls, and notes delight my soul.

I have heard scores of beautiful bird songs, though none as hauntingly evocative as that of the wood thrush and the hermit thrush. The males of both species produce an ethereal flute-like song that reverberates through the forest over great distances. The timbre, or vocal quality, is similar in both birds, but the phrasing and melody are distinctive. Upon hearing the first notes, time and space disappear, and I am transported to a different realm.

The wood thrush is slightly smaller than a robin, which is also in the thrush family and sings a most pleasing song. While a robin enjoys the open spaces and tree-lined edges of suburban backyards, the wood thrush chooses to make its home in damp, deciduous forests composed of tall leaf laden trees. It thrives in the shelter of shrubs, wildflowers, ferns, and vines that make up the understory below. The cinnamon-brown back of the wood thrush blends perfectly with its surroundings, making it difficult to locate even after hearing its song. However, if you have found the general area and quietly wait, eyes alert, you will often be rewarded. Typically, wood thrushes search the leaf litter on the forest floor for food items. Here they find invertebrates by turning over leaves and digging through debris with their beaks and feet. On occasion, when one lifts its head, it is possible to see a distinct white ring circling each eye and striking black spots on its beige breast.

You are more likely to hear a wood thrush than to see one. Listening to its voice, Henry David Thoreau wrote: "It changes all hours to an eternal morning." Singing from the lower canopy, the centerpiece of the song is often described simply as "ee-oh-lay." While these are the commonly heard notes of its song, there is much more to appreciate about the vocalization of the wood thrush. In fact, it has the unique ability to sing two notes at once. Its voice box, or syrinx, is equipped with two sets of vocal cords that it can operate independently. In the third and final phase of its three-part song, you can hear an internal duet as the bird harmonizes with itself.

After spending the winter in the lowland rainforests of Central America, the wood thrush returns to our North American forests in spring. The males, arriving first in late April or early May, establish territories which they announce and defend vocally. Several days later, when the females arrive, courtship begins. Upon identifying the female of his choosing, the male pursues her as she leads him in circular flights around the trees. Intermittently they stop to perch together on a tree branch, where the fluttering of wings may briefly occur, until the chase begins anew.

Once mated, the wood thrush pair is monogamous, raising the young together and later mating, if conditions allow, for a second nesting. Unlike some birds, which take the same mate for their lifetime, a wood thrush pair remain together for one season only. The female chooses the nest site and builds the nest, often in the forks of understory trees or bushes. Laying a foundation of larger leaves, then weaving in grasses and rootlets, she uses mud to secure the layers one to the other. Using her breast and belly, she pushes out the sides of the nest forming a small bowl into which she deposits three to four turquoise green eggs. The female will incubate the eggs for thirteen to fourteen days. Both male and female take on the duties of feeding the young once they have hatched. Eventually, the male takes on more of this duty as the female starts a second brood.

The wood thrush is the official bird of the District of Columbia. They are frequently heard in Rock Creek Park, the 1,754-acre national park within our nation's capital. Unfortunately, wood thrush populations are currently in decline. Over the last several decades, their ability to reproduce has been significantly impacted. Loss of their signature habitat—mature forests—to the development of housing tracts and commercial enterprises has led to forest fragmentation, which cannot support healthy populations. Additionally, nest parasitism, a behavior carried out by the brown-headed cowbird, has had a negative impact on the wood thrush. Brown-headed cowbirds do not make a nest. Instead, they lay their eggs in the nests of other birds including those of the wood thrush. Often the cowbirds will toss the eggs of the wood thrush out of the nest, leaving the unsuspecting thrush to raise the cowbird young as their own. Cowbird hatchlings grow quickly and are often aggressive toward nest mates, frequently pushing "siblings" out of the nest.

The robin's cheerful dawn song and the wood thrush's fluid melody are true standouts on a summer's day. Their vocal quality seemed unrivalled until I heard something new on an island in Maine. On this day, I led a group of campers on a cross-island trail shaded by spruce and fir trees. What we saw mid-trail stopped everyone. The narrow trail led to an expansive opening in the forest where every rock, stump, and root was carpeted with emerald green mosses, soft and inviting. Tall spire-shaped spruce and fir trees swayed in the salt air breezes high above us. We decided that we needed to stay—even for a short while—to experience this place. Each of us chose a solitary moss-covered boulder as a resting place. Once we quieted, the forest filled again with the sounds of gulls, terns, and wind rocking the trees. Then, a song like none other filled this extraordinary place. It turned out to be a hermit thrush whose vibrant melodic phrases captured our spirits. Such a little bird, such a big voice! For a full twenty minutes the hermit thrush shared its liquid notes.

The song starts with a sustained whistle, followed by three or four notes at different pitches. The descending musical phrases progress to a minor key, which some describe as melancholy. When the crystal-clear voice of a hermit thrush echoes through the trees, we are gifted moments of unparalleled beauty.

Unlike the wood thrush, the hermit thrush prefers coniferous forests with its spruce, fir, and pine. Slightly smaller than a wood thrush, the hermit thrush is best recognized by its bold reddish tail. It is known for raising its tail and slowly bobbing it up and down while flicking its wings. The head and back are a rich brown, while the underparts show clear spots on the throat and blurred spots on the breast. After spending the winter in the southern states or Central America, the hermit thrush arrives in the northeast in early spring and sticks around longer in the fall than most other migrants. Recognized as the state bird of Vermont, the hermit thrush can be found throughout the northern tier of North America in spring and summer. Occasionally, birds will remain for the winter. Typically, they will make cup-like nests out of grasses, twigs, ferns, lichen, mud, and bark fibers. They can be found nesting at the base of spruce trees or dried fern beds on the ground, although they will sometimes nest low in the trees and shrubs.

The vocal acumen of the hermit thrush is mentioned in the poetry of Walt Whitman and T. S. Elliott. American composer Amy Beach, inspired by this lyrical bird, incorporated its song in her orchestral works "Hermit Thrush at Dawn" and "Hermit Thrush at Eve." As a child with perfect pitch, she would frequently transcribe bird songs into musical notes, eventually using the song of the hermit thrush as the centerpiece of her most famous compositions.

An Oneida Nation story, told to teach the value of honesty, describes a time long ago when the Creator called all the birds to a great council. The Creator offered to give each bird their own song based on how high they could fly. The most beautiful songs would be given to those that flew to the highest heights. There was a little brown thrush who realized it had little chance against the largest birds, so it developed a plan. It flew onto an eagle's head and buried itself beneath the feathers. The eagle flew far beyond all the other birds until finally exhausted it descended to earth. The little thrush, fully rested, hopped off the eagle's head and began his own upward flight until he arrived at a hole in the sky where he heard a beautiful song. He stayed in this place until he knew the song by heart and then flew back to earth. As he approached the council rock around which the other birds had gathered, he realized they were glaring at him because he had cheated. Rather than return to the council to face the eagle and be shamed by others for his dishonesty, the thrush flew into the deep woods and hid in the trees. This is why the hermit thrush is seldom seen.

Since my first experience with the hermit thrush, I have been fortunate to hear it on several more occasions. When the hermit thrush and I are in the same stretch of the north woods, my cares slip away and I am mindful only of its ethereal sound. My wife, Trudy, whose encounters mirror my own, set feelings to verse:

Hermit Thrush

When you sing ~
We are spellbound

When you sing ~
Souls open wide

When you sing ~
You fill the forest

Vocal wonder, priceless joy!

Dining at the Bank

"Spout at three o'clock!" Everyone races to the bow of the boat, binoculars in hand. Jostling for a good sight line, we search the water off the starboard side. Suddenly, an immense black head pierces the surface. A long white flipper trails alongside its sleek, muscular body. A collective cry of surprise soars into the air. Cameras click, binoculars focus. An adult humpback whale glides calmly alongside the boat. Its bulbous head and broad body are only yards away from us. Seconds later, the whale arches its back, lifts its tail high into the air, and slides headfirst into the depths. The last things we see are the white markings and wavy rear edges of its tail. This is a sounding dive.

Four times a day during the summer months, whale watching boats depart from Provincetown on Cape Cod in search of the great leviathans. Six miles north of Race Point lighthouse, an underwater ridge known as Stellwagen Bank rises from the ocean floor. Named after Commander Henry Stellwagen who mapped the area in 1854 and 1855, the bank extends north to northwest in the direction of Cape Ann, encompassing 842 square miles. The waters of Stellwagen Bank are shallow and unusually productive, a result of frequent surface turnover in the water column. Colder nutrient rich water moving along the ocean floor, meets the bank and is pushed up to mix with the warmer surface water. This turnover both oxygenates and cycles nutrients necessary to feed the abundant plankton in the area. In turn, the plankton becomes food for small fish which then become food for larger animals. This underwater landscape, formed by the retreat of the glaciers, is renowned for its biological diversity and productivity. April through October, Stellwagen is one of the world's premier whale watching locations. In 1992 the area was designated a National Marine Sanctuary.

Seventeen species of whales have been sighted on the bank, but the finback and humpback whales dominate the scene. These "morning mowers," as the author Herman Melville called them, plow through the brine, devouring several tons of fish each day. In the absence of teeth, these whales never grasp or chew their food. Whatever they eat, they swallow alive and whole.

The finbacks and humpbacks are classified in a group of giant whales called the mysticetes, or mustached whales. The upper jaw of a mysticete is lined with a series of thin fibrous plates called baleen which separate food from water, much like a strainer. The throat and chest contain a series of pleated furrows, which expand many times over as the whale feeds. With its mouth wide open, it takes in an enormous amount of water, containing hundreds of schooling fish. Closing its mouth, the whale pushes the water out through its baleen plates, capturing and swallowing the fish.

The primary food source in Stellwagen Bank is the sand lance, a four-to-six-inch silvery fish. A popular bait fish for fishermen, sand lance burrow deep into the sandy bottom at night. During the day, they travel in giant schools, comprising thousands of individual fish. They resemble eels as they swim with a slithering wavelike motion. When opportunity arises, the whales feed on mackerel, herring, menhaden, capelin, and krill.

Finbacks are the second largest whales in the world and some of the fastest. Though their numbers are improving, they remain on the endangered species list with an estimated population of 100,000 individuals worldwide. The tall forceful spout of this species makes it easy to spot from a distance. Sleek and streamlined, the finback moves through the water at a velocity that matches the top speed of whale-watching vessels. Colored black above and white below, the color pattern is broken by a chevron blaze along the side and a white section on the right side of the lips and baleen. The white patch on the mouth is thought to help attract fish.

When feeding, a finback will lunge headlong into a school of fish traveling at top speed. The fish, taken by surprise, have little chance to escape. The whale will then turn on its side, allowing water and fish to stream in and out of its mouth. Spying the plight of the captured fish, gulls and seabirds often dive right into the whale's mouth to grab a free meal. For a long time, scientists wondered how a whale could take in so much water at one time without choking. Recent studies reveal that baleen whales have a specialized throat plug which enables them to keep these huge amounts of water relegated solely to their throat pouches. Though finbacks usually feed at the surface, I have seen a finback rise with sand in its mouth following a feeding foray along the bottom.

Truly, the humpbacks are the stars of whale-watching trips. I spent a summer working as a naturalist on a whale watching boat, narrating two trips to Stellwagen Bank every day. During that time, I learned to recognize individual whales and observe some of their unique behaviors, including breaching (when a whale jumps completely out of the water), flipper slapping (the raising of a pectoral fin at a ninety degree angle and rapidly smacking it down on the water), lob-tailing (raising its flukes to slap them forcefully on the water's surface), and spy hopping (when a whale positions itself vertically, eyes above the water, to inspect its surroundings).

Humpbacks seen in action never disappoint eager whale watchers. At times appearing slow and stocky, they would swim right beside the boats. Their broad heads are dotted with knoblike tubercles, each containing a single hair used to detect prey. The early whalers thought these knobs looked like they were holding the whale's head together and referred to them as "stove bolts." Their long, white flippers, characteristic only to humpbacks, measure approximately a third of the whale's body length. The spout is broad and bushy, reaching a height approaching three meters. Sounding dives and lob-tailing expose unique patterns on the undersides of a humpback's flukes which scientists use to identify individual whales.

In the 1970s, researchers with Allied Whale at the College of the Atlantic in Maine developed a photo-id system for identifying individual humpback whales. Based on distinctive field marks found on the flukes, these marks, like our fingerprints, are specific to each individual whale. Occasionally, there are other identifiable features on the dorsal fins or other parts of the body, though these are not often as visible. Once named, an individual's activity is easier to monitor as it moves through the ocean waters. Through tracking their movements, researchers learned that the whales seen in Stellwagen Bank spend their winters in the West Indies, where the water is warmer for mating and raising their calves. They return to their northern haunts every spring seeking the abundance of food found in the North Atlantic's colder waters. The first North Atlantic Humpback Whale Catalog was published in 1977 by Allied Whale and included 120 individuals. Over forty years later, this same catalog now lists 10,000 individuals. This catalog includes whales found in every major feeding ground in the North Atlantic, and includes detailed information on birth, gender, migration routes, health, and death of individual whales. In 1981, a similar catalog was developed for finback whales containing information relating to 800 individuals.

I have observed a variety of feeding strategies employed by humpback whales. I have seen them stun and disorient prey by slapping them with their flippers or flukes. At times, they engage in bubble-net feeding which involves several whales working together. One whale takes the lead, diving deep beneath a school of fish and releasing a steady stream of tiny bubbles through its blowhole. The other whales surround the fish and swim in a spiral pattern, preventing their escape. Surrounded by a wall of bubbles and whales on all sides, the agitated fish school tightly together. Upon reaching the surface, the whales swim through the school, mouths open wide, then filter the water through their baleen plates. Lunge feeding was the most dramatic technique I observed, which is employed by all the baleen whales.

Once I began to recognize individual whales, I noticed that some had developed their own specialized feeding techniques. One would jump completely out of the water, landing forcefully, stunning the fish. Next, it would blow a bubble cloud and then rise into the middle of the cloud, its mouth wide open. There was another whale I had become familiar with who turned upside down before surface feeding. Was it scanning the water to determine where the fish might be? After backing into the water, it would emerge minutes later, lunging through a bubble cloud.

Populations of humpback and finback whales were once on the verge of extinction due to commercial and factory whaling. In 1986, the International Whaling Commission banned the hunting of whales except for those taken by indigenous tribes for food and those used for scientific research. Fortunately, this moratorium allowed the humpback and finback populations to begin recovery. Humpback whales are currently listed as a species of least concern, with a global population between 120,000 and 150,000 individuals. However, in addition to hunting, whales face a variety of threats including vessel strikes, entanglement with fishing gear, offshore gas and oil exploration, harassment, pollution, underwater noise, and climate change, which impacts the ocean temperature and prey distribution. It is encouraging to know that progress has been made toward the protection of some species. However, more responsible and thoughtful interventions must be implemented to ensure the health of all earth's miraculous creatures.

The captain spies a patch of green frothy bubbles on the port side of our boat. Eyes peeled, we turn to focus our binoculars and cameras on that spot. Suddenly, a humpback whale lunges through the bubble cloud with its mouth agape. I can see the whale's enormous tongue against the roof of its mouth centered between rows of baleen. I am mere yards away from one of the largest mammals on earth. Fifty million years ago, its ancestors lived on land. Millions of years later, whales evolved to become ocean dwelling creatures. Spending time with these awe-inspiring giants of the sea excites me to my core. I return again and again.

Life in Constant Motion

"Imagine. There is a mammal in these woods with a heart beat like a hummingbird and a musky smell like a skunk. It locates prey using echolocation like a bat and paralyzes it with venomous saliva like a rattlesnake."

Eyes wide, the campers were hooked. I asked them to form a circle and remain in place. Leaving the circle, I walked back to the area where I spotted a dead animal a few feet off the trail. Picking it up, I rejoined the campers. Holding it in my cupped hands, I stepped into the middle of the circle and slowly walked around so each child could see it closely. Resembling a mouse with a pointed snout and short tail, this was the first time any of them had ever seen a shrew. Several campers excitedly told me they had read about shrews in the Redwall fantasy series penned by Brian Jacques.

Although it is one of the most abundant mammals in North America, few people ever see them. They are tiny, secretive, and rare to find above ground. Easily mistaken for a mouse, when examined side by side, their differences are undeniable. Like all rodents, a mouse has two pairs of large front teeth, called incisors, followed by a toothless gap on each side of the jaw, ending in a set of grinding teeth, or molars. A mouse uses its incisors to gnaw on roots and grains. The shrew, on the other hand, is an insectivore, possessing thirty-two sharp biting teeth for grasping, ripping, and tearing its prey into edible pieces. Its diet consists primarily of insects and also includes a variety of other small animals, including other shrews. As a popular prey item, the world of a mouse is a dangerous one. Not so for the predaceous shrew, which is akin to a fierce little tiger, unafraid to face the most difficult odds and capable of killing a mouse twice its size and weight.

If you had the rare opportunity to see a shrew, chances are it was a dead one left on your doorstep as a gift from your dog or cat. At first glance a shrew's appearance can confuse predators. Hawks, owls, weasels, foxes, and snakes prey on shrews, but once caught, often abandon them. When confronted, a shrew can activate the release of a strong-smelling musk stored in glands located on each of its flanks. This musky smelling fluid produces a rank taste, rendering the shrew repulsive.

One of the shrew's most distinguishing features is its snout, a highly developed olfactory tool essential for detecting food items. Coupled with its keen sense of touch, these sensory tools compensate for its lack of visual acuity. Life under the ground requires little more than the sensing of dark and light. Here also, in much the same way as bats, shrews use their unique ability to echolocate as they maneuver around tree roots, avoid obstructions, and locate a meal. Their ears, hidden beneath the fur, might lead us to think that hearing is a weaker sense when actually it is surprisingly acute, serving them well when challenges arise. When alarmed shrews emit a high-pitched squeal, it may not be audible to the human ear as many of their vocalizations are so high in pitch that they are undetectable.

Two common species of shrews in the northeast are the masked shrew, whose average weight is one-fifth of an ounce, and the northern short-tailed shrew, which averages half an ounce. The tiniest mammal on the North American continent is the pigmy shrew, whose body measures about two inches in length and weighs in at one-fourteenth of an ounce, about as much as a dime. The water shrew can be found both above and under the water. A capable swimmer, it can hold its breath for fifteen seconds assisting it in a successful hunt. The webbed third and fourth toes and hairy fringe on its hind feet make it possible for the water shrew to walk or glide on water for a short distance. Acting much like a

hydrofoil, the shrew is supported by a collection of air molecules which build up in the fringes.

A young shrew begins life in a small circular nest made of grasses and leaves. It might be situated in a hollow stump, under a log, or in a vacant shallow burrow. An average litter consists of six or seven blind, helpless, and naked little beings, about the size of a honeybee. They grow quickly and are fully furred within two weeks. In a month, they are full-grown and pushed out of the nest. From then on, each of the young shrew siblings leads a solitary adult life.

Though most animals are either diurnal or nocturnal, a shrew is active twenty-four hours a day. In addition, they remain active all four seasons of the year. Constantly on the move, a shrew sleeps for no more than two minutes at a time. I have read that a heart beats, within all creatures regardless of size, approximately two billion times in their lifetime. The average human heart rate is seventy beats per minute, enabling humans to live for 80 years or more. The average shrew heart beats over a thousand times per minute. They are considered old on their first birthday, and it is rare for one to live beyond two years.

Hunting and eating are the main activities of daily life. Due to the shrew's high rate of metabolism, large quantities of food must be consumed, requiring it to eat three times its body weight each day. If I ate three times my weight in a day, I would need to eat 450 pounds of food in twenty-four hours. Shrews feed primarily on insects, occasionally eating earthworms, salamanders, snakes, tiny songbirds, mice, moles, and, in fact, other shrews. Its voracious appetite, out of proportion to its size, is often beneficial to other species as they keep some insect pests under control. This has been the case in New Brunswick, Canada where shrews destroyed sixty percent of a larch sawfly population in a few days, avoiding the devastation of adjacent acres of larch trees in the area.

Like the duck-billed platypus and the vampire bat, shrews are classified as venomous mammals. They produce venom in their salivary glands. Ready when needed to ward off challengers, the shrew can deposit this paralyzing venom through its bite. Unlike a poisonous snake which injects venom through its fangs as it bites, a shrew's venom is mixed with saliva, rendering it less potent. The shrews bite must break through the skin exposing the area to the saliva. Although their bite is deadly to mice, most humans will only experience some discomfort. Few people have ever been bitten by a shrew, for the shrew keeps its distance and avoids people at all costs. One scientist was bitten on a finger while handling a short-tailed shrew. He felt a burning sensation thirty seconds later. The area around the puncture swelled and became whitish, and the burning sensation traveled up his arm to his elbow. All inflammation disappeared in a matter of days.

Late summer into fall is the best time to see a live shrew as it is busily preparing for winter. Many years ago on an October morning, I spotted a short-tailed shrew running across the forest trail. I put on my heavy gloves, caught the shrew, and brought it inside to a large terrarium complete with plants, water, and a foot and a half of soil. My plan was to keep it for a few days of observation and then let it go. Mealworms, crickets, grasshoppers, ants, and any other insects I could find went into the terrarium. I supplemented its insect diet with peanut butter, sunflower seeds, and other concentrated foods. Although I never observed the shrew eating, the food always disappeared. Later, after I had released it, I dug underneath the soil, where I found a large cache of food in one corner of the tank. So secretive was my guest, that I rarely saw it. On one occasion, I decided to check the interior by gently moving some of the plants around. A loud high-pitched squeal shocked me and I withdrew my hand immediately. Weighing less than an ounce, I knew the shrew to be a formidable creature and heeded its warning. Over the next few days, I learned what I could about its behavior without invading its privacy. On the third day, I took the shrew back to the area where I'd found it and set it free.

Shrews may eat in captivity, but they will not breed under these conditions. Since they prefer staying underground, they cannot be observed in a terrarium. Understandably, they are viciously protective when handled and their venomous saliva is dangerous. While Shakespeare is regarded as the greatest playwright of all time, I have qualms about his characterization of a shrew. Anyone that has studied or observed these fascinating animals knows there is no taming of a shrew.

Aquatic Engineers

Several summers ago, I had the good fortune to spend a week canoeing and camping with a group in the Boundary Waters of northern Minnesota. Every morning, we woke to billowing clouds of mist rising from the water and each day was packed with sights and information that only a paddling excursion could reveal. At night, we gazed into star-studded skies, mesmerized on occasion by the swirling green curtains of the Aurora Borealis. Loon calls permeated the evening air with ethereal wails, tremolos, and yodels. And often, to our delight, we spied beavers; some swimming and feeding, others engaged in their latest engineering project.

The largest rodent in North America, the beaver is a stout-bodied animal with thick, glossy brown fur and a long, flat, hairless tail, resembling a paddle. The tail supports the beaver when its stands erect, serves as a rudder and propeller when swimming in the water, and communicates danger or aggression. During a twilight paddle, we were startled by a loud thwack on the water near our canoe. A beaver slapped its tail on the water's surface warning us that we were too close. We took the hint, paddled in the opposite direction and gave the beaver its space.

Beaver tracks can sometimes be hard to detect. Dragging its tail as it walks, tracks in the mud or loose sandy soil can be easily erased. Those that escape erasure reveal a sizeable difference between the hind and front feet. The hindfeet, six to seven inches long, are fully webbed for swimming and provide stability in the mud. The webless forefeet, two to three inches long, feature strong claws, perfect for digging, carrying mud, holding food, and combing through their fur. When grooming their fur, they apply an oily substance called castoreum, which is secreted from their anal glands, giving the fur its waterproof properties. Castoreum is also used in combination with urine to mark territory.

Their impressively large front teeth are perfect tools for cutting through layers of wood. Their front teeth continually grow throughout their lives and depend on daily use to manage their size. The orange color on the outer layers of the teeth is due to the iron infused within them. When underwater, their lips close behind the incisors, allowing them to carry branches and sticks without taking on a mouthful of water. Strict vegetarians, beavers feed on aquatic plants, along with the twigs and bark of small succulent trees like willow, aspen, poplar, and birch. Beavers gnaw on trees until they fall and stash branches underwater near their lodges, storing food for leaner times.

Beavers are master builders and excavators, constructing dams, lodges, burrows, and canals. Using logs, sticks, rocks and mud, the dams are designed to maintain a constant water level. Once established, they can depend on sufficient underwater access to their lodges and winter food supply. Equipped with at least two underwater passageways leading to a large central chamber, the lodges can be free-standing or built up against a bank. Building materials are packed tightly together and plastered with mud, completely shutting out any vestiges of light. Creatures of darkness, beavers spend their days in their lodges emerging during the twilight and nighttime hours.

Beavers mate for life and live in family units called colonies. A typical colony consists of two adult parents, the yearlings born the previous year, and the kits of the current year. In their social hierarchy, the adult female is dominant. The young are typically born in May or June following a four-month gestation period. After two years, any young who have not already left on their own are driven out by their parents. On average, the young travel five to seven miles to establish a new territory.

Beavers played a major role in the European exploration and settlement of North America. For centuries, the thick, soft, waterproof fur was prized for hats and trimmings. The oldest corporation in North America, the Hudson Bay Company, was built on trading and selling furs, and beaver pelts were their most sought-after item. By the end of the 1800s, uncontrolled trapping and habitat destruction nearly wiped out a once thriving population of beavers. During the twentieth century, laws were passed to protect the species and beavers from Canada were reintroduced to our eastern states. Today, the population is large and stable, although it is a tiny fraction of what it was when the colonists arrived. Aside from desert regions in the southwest, beavers can be found throughout the United States and Canada. In recent years, I've seen signs of beaver activity in urban and suburban locations. On a field trip with students to the Fairmount Waterworks in Philadelphia, Pennsylvania, we found gnawed branches and cut tree stumps at the edge of the Schuylkill River, clear signs of beaver activity.

On occasion, beavers build their structures in places that interfere with public safety. At Marsh Creek State Park in southeastern Pennsylvania, beavers built a dam in front of a spillway. After workers dismantled the dam, the beavers built another one, this time near a water level gauge, rendering the readings inaccurate. The beavers were trapped and relocated. At nearby French Creek State Park, beavers have flourished for over twenty years with little concern. For the most part, their labeling as a nuisance is a function of human constructs.

Much like humans, beavers alter existing environments. Depending on your perspective, beavers simultaneously harm and protect aquatic communities. On the one hand, beavers cut down trees and change the course of streams. At the same time, they create ponds, restore waterways, mitigate droughts and floods, enhance groundwater recharge, and improve wildlife habitat for many species. They help purify the water by slowing the flow and allowing sediment to settle before going downstream. The pool of water behind every dam improves habitat for bass, while trout endure the loss of cold, fast-moving water. Of course, the beavers have their own agenda and are not concerned about our preferences.

Kayaking at a nearby lake, I enjoy looking for signs of beaver activity. In a remote portion of the lake, inaccessible to larger boats, there is a beaver lodge that's been built into the bank. Fresh saplings, their light-yellow ends sporting chew marks, lay on top, indicating that this is an active lodge. Nearby, there are additional signs of beaver activity including nibbled twigs, partially gnawed tree trunks, and felled trees. I have yet to see the beavers that live here, so I imagine them sleeping inside. Paddling away from the lodge, I think back to my beaver encounters on the Boundary Waters. Things will be different here in a few hours. They are waiting for twilight, just like the beavers further north.

Go for the Gold

It is a warm mid-August day and goldfinches seem to be everywhere at once. A bright yellow male lands on a purple coneflower, bending the stalk and plucking seeds from the flower head. Another male arrives to inspect a nearby patch of Black-eyed Susans growing near the birdbath where several more are busy splashing. Up in the trees, vocal young flutter their wings, begging for food. Only a month ago, our local goldfinch population maintained a quiet presence. Today, their strident calls proclaim the vigor of new generations.

By this time in August, many of our local birds have molted, exchanging colorful, worn feathers for subtler, newer ones. They have mated, nested, and raised young weeks ago. In contrast, the American goldfinch synchronizes nesting with the availability of food needed to feed its brood. Birds of prey nest earlier in the year, taking advantage of peak numbers in the rodent population, while many songbirds gear up for late spring and early summer when the insect world is in full swing. As a granivore, the goldfinch feeds primarily on seeds, gathered and split with its strong conical bill. In the spring, seeds from catkin-bearing trees and shrubs and the occasional insect form the bulk of their diet. However, these are inadequate for feeding young. Plants with fibrous seeds, including sunflowers and thistles, are robust beginning in the latter half of July and throughout the month of August. They produce both nesting material and food needed to feed nestlings.

Courtship and pairing, involving flight displays and song, take place during the months of April and May. The canary yellow male with his black cap and black and white wing and tail markings most often catches our eye. However, it is the female that must be impressed, and her criteria includes more than just flashy colors. Often a series of short chases ensues, the male pursuing the female. At times, two males may chase each other with the female picking the dominant of the two. Once paired, they join other goldfinches, creating small groups often seen feeding together. One July day, my wife looked up from working at the kitchen sink to see who might be visiting the birdfeeders outside the window. At first glance, it appeared that our side yard was in motion. Closer examination revealed a small flock of goldfinches busily feeding among the dandelions in the tall grass.

As nesting time approaches, the pair begins to search for a well-protected site. This usually involves locating two or three vertical branches within a sapling or shrub to which a nest can be secured. Interestingly, mated pairs often nest near each other, perhaps indicating a preference for safety in numbers. Nest building is the sole work of the female who weaves together a tidy cup of pliable plant fibers, including strips of bark and vines. She lines the interior, which is approximately two inches in diameter, with softer materials such as thistle, milkweed, and cattail down. Threads from spider and caterpillar webs are used to secure the nest to twigs and small branches in the fork of the tree or shrub. When complete, goldfinch nests are so structurally sound that many can hold water, posing a potential problem for young should there be periods of extended rainfall.

Soon after nest construction, the female settles in to incubate four to six pale bluish-white eggs. Flying overhead, the male regularly returns and responds to her hunger calls with partially digested meals of seeds. The female spends approximately two weeks on the nest protecting her eggs. Occasionally she leaves the nest, her absence creating opportunity for a brown-headed cowbird to quickly lay an egg and leave before the female returns. The cowbird's choice is a poor one. Once hatched, its young cannot survive the vegetarian diet of the goldfinch.

The task of feeding the young is shared by both male and female. Regurgitated seed, thistle being top choice, "fills the bill." In eleven to seventeen days, the young are ready to leave the nest. They exercise their flight muscles and begin life on the wing. At this time, they can be seen flying in pursuit of their parents, begging for food. I watched a goldfinch parent besieged by four fledglings beating their wings, insisting they be fed. As a parent myself, I imagine this adult may have other goals in mind for its young. Their survival depends on their ability to find food and feed themselves.

From my deck, I watch a goldfinch fly across the backyard, rising and falling in shallow waves: a yellow flash, repeating its four-syllable flight call, "perchickory" or "potato chip." Antonio Vivaldi's Concerto for Flute in D, also known as the "Goldfinch," was inspired by their numerous vocalizations. The piece does not attempt to copy the bird note for note, but rather captures the essence of the bird's beautiful warbles and trills. Each song variation has a distinct purpose. There are specific songs associated with courtship, setting up territories, protecting the nest, and feeding, among other activities. Goldfinches are also known to incorporate other bird's songs into their repertoire.

Goldfinches thrive in weedy fields, where thistles and other members of the Asteraceae family are common. They have adapted well to suburban lawns and other cultivated areas. Active and acrobatic, you can frequently find a goldfinch upside down or sideways on the seed heads of flowers during the summer months. Dainty and light, it weighs only eleven to twenty grams, less than an ounce or about the weight of a compact disc. During the winter months, goldfinches are frequent visitors at bird feeders. The most successful way to attract a goldfinch to your feeders is to put out nyjer seed. Although commonly sold as thistle, the tiny black seeds are from the guizotia flower, native to Africa. Nyger exposed to winter's wet, snowy weather combined with infrequent warmer days can quickly lead to seed spoilage. Once rancid, the goldfinches will avoid it. Checking regularly and dumping undesirable seed will assure continued visitation.

The American goldfinch is the only finch in North America that molts completely twice a year. During the September postnuptial molt, it sheds a few feathers at a time, gradually exchanging bright yellow feathers for an understated palette of brown, olive, or chartreuse. The female maintains her earth-tone colors throughout the year, although she molts just like her counterpart. The best way to tell the males and females apart during the winter season is to focus on the flight feathers, which are jet-black for the males and less lustrous for the females. In spring, the prenuptial molt prepares them for the breeding season. The male's eye-catching colors return, increasing his ability to attract a mate. Carotenoid pigments found in plants contribute to his colorful appearance.

Late summer is prime time for watching these colorful birds. The juveniles are busy practicing the art of flight and finding food, and now that nesting is over, the adults are out and in the open. Some migrate to warmer climes in mid-autumn, while many are winter residents. On cold snowy days, they might burrow in the snow to create a sleeping cavity or roost closely together in evergreen trees to stay warm. It is always a treat to see them when they come out to feed. Sometimes referred to as "the wild canary of the Americas," goldfinches are so appealing that three different states, New Jersey, Iowa, and Washington, have adopted the American goldfinch as their state bird.

This morning, the vitality of the goldfinches holds me fast. I can't take my eyes off their quick movements. Yellow flashes spring from the grass; insistent young pursue their parent; the waters of the birdbath are alive with males and females. It is the kind of morning I can't wait to share. Time to text my neighbor. Bird alert!

Life in a Box

My lesson was supposed to be about insects. Every year, the second grade begins the school year with a thematic study of insects, integrating science and language arts. I had every intention of sticking with the theme. Before class, I headed out to scout the trail. I wanted to make sure there were ample signs of insect activity. As anticipated, there was an abundance of evidence including a variety of sounds and live sightings within the first fifty feet. Confident I'd chosen the right path, I headed back to my classroom and waited for my students.

At first, the lesson went as planned, eighteen pairs of eyes spotting insect evidence everywhere we looked. They were eager and determined to search every square inch of the trail. Not far into the woods, however, our insect exploration came to an abrupt halt followed by a series of high-pitched squeals which led to a student stampede. They had spotted a box turtle lumbering its way through leaves and over twigs. They were thrilled. We formed a large circle around the turtle to give everyone a clear view. Rapid-fire questions leapt into the air. I fielded them as quickly as I could though children's questions often leave adults speechless. "That's a great question. Let's do some research when we get back to class," I'd reply. We were so focused on the turtle that the world around us disappeared. On that serendipitous morning, the box turtle in the middle of our circle was the only thing that mattered. Everything else could wait.

Fossil evidence informs us that turtles were present on the earth approximately 230 million years ago, since the age of the first dinosaurs. The oldest known box turtle fossils, found in Nebraska, date back to the Miocene epoch, fifteen million years ago. The secret to their success lies in the development of their most identifiable feature: the shell. Inhabiting a body shaped as a refuge, turtles can escape the attacks of predators and untold dangers.

A turtle's shell is connected to all parts of its body. The ribs and backbones are fused into the bone of the carapace or upper shell. Its front and back leg girdles form separate attachments to the carapace. A protective layer of scutes covers the carapace, adding durability to the shell. These plate-like scutes are formed by layers of a protein called keratin, a substance also found in our fingernails. Land turtles like the eastern box turtle add a new layer of keratinized material each year to compensate for wear. When the new material is lain down, it moves beyond the previous year's growth, forming concentric rings. Counting these rings can provide a good estimate of an individual's age until it stops growing, between the ages of twelve and twenty. After that, it is harder to estimate the age beyond looking at the wear and tear of the shell.

The shell located underneath the body of a turtle is called the plastron. It acts as a shield, protecting the turtle as it moves through and over its environment. Along its sides, the carapace and the plastron are fused together by a bony structure known as the bridge, affording further protection for soft inner organs and connective tissue. It is on the plastron of the eastern box turtle where we find a hinge. The combination of a highly domed carapace on top and a hinge on the bottom, allows the turtle to withdraw completely inside the shell and close tightly. Predators, who continue to bite at it, swat it or even try to dig it out of the shell, soon move on in search of an easier target. Transformed from potential prey to impenetrable container, the box turtle lives on another day.

Eastern box turtles are omnivores. They eat berries, mushrooms, fruits, slugs, snails, earthworms, and a variety of other invertebrates. Carrion

is also on their menu. They do not chew their food as they do not have teeth. Instead, their mouths are shaped more like a beak and feature sharp bony edges perfect for shearing and tearing their food into digestible pieces.

Eastern box turtles are primarily terrestrial, living most of their lives in moist woodlands. They do not have the webbing between their toes found on aquatic turtles and the shape of their bodies more closely resembles that of their close relative, the land-dwelling tortoise. Surprisingly, box turtles have been observed swimming, but they usually enter the water just to soak and wade. They are often found on hot summer days resting in the shallows of a pond or stream.

There are a few easy ways to determine the sex of box turtles. Although there is a lot of variation, the eyes on the males range from orange to bright red, while the eyes of the female are yellow, brown or ochre. The male's plastron features a concave indentation that flares outward to meet the edges of its carapace. This indentation allows the male to securely mount the female to mate. The female's hinged plastron is smooth and flat in comparison. Both males and females have claws on each foot that provide secure footing as they move among leaf litter, grasses, and rocks. A female box turtle's back claws are longer, straighter and thicker for digging into a chosen nest site. Both male and female box turtle shells are covered in a variety of striking patterns in shades of brown, orange and yellow. It seems that no two turtles are patterned alike although there is little doubt about their species.

Most of the year, box turtles lead a solitary life, paying little attention to other turtles in the area. In most cases, an individual spends its entire life within a 250-yard radius. When the territory of a female overlaps with that of a male, mating can take place. Neither will stray beyond their individual boundaries to locate a potential mate. This can be a significant limiting factor when turtle populations are diminished.

Box turtles have a single clutch of two to eight eggs in a nest that is several inches deep. Once the female has excavated her nest in sand or soft soil and laid her eggs, she will leave them to be nurtured by the elements. In many turtle species, including the box turtle, the temperature within the substrate surrounding their eggs determines the gender of the offspring. Eggs located deep inside the core will differ in temperature from those on the outer edge. Warmer temperatures favor the development of female turtles. Cooler temperatures give rise to more males. Eggs that survive predation and incursions hatch in two months. Once hatched, the first task of the young is to dig their way to the surface. Setting off alone, each quarter-sized hatchling grows quickly, reaching their full size in five to six years. It takes approximately five years for young box turtles to develop the plastron's moveable hinge.

As a child, I would find box turtles on a regular basis in my backyard and at my summer day camp. I'll never forget the moments I shared with them when we looked at each other eye to eye. Today, spotting a box turtle is rare. They are listed as a species of special concern in Pennsylvania, Connecticut, Massachusetts, New Hampshire, and Michigan. The state of Maine has placed them on their endangered list. They are listed as a vulnerable species by the International Union of Conservation of Nature (IUCN)—one of the world's leading conservation organizations. Box turtle populations have suffered greatly from habitat destruction. When their homes are destroyed by development, they are separated from their familiar territories and become disoriented. They have trouble finding food, wander into unknown dangers, and suffer deteriorating health.

Threats to the lives of box turtles are numerous. One of the biggest threats is the illegal pet trade. Box turtles purchased from pet stores are often species from other countries. Unfortunately, some owners tire of caring for them and some need to move and cannot take the turtles to their new location. There are others who decide to release their pet turtle into the wild. Introduced to a new outdoor habitat, a non-native turtle can potentially spread disease and weaken the gene pool. A better solution would be to surrender the turtle to an organization which knows how to care for it, like an animal rescue or rehab center.

Individuals with good intentions sometimes cause more harm than good when "rescuing" wild box turtles and deciding to keep them as pets. Box turtles have a specific home territory and seldom wander more than a few hundred yards in either direction. If released into a new location, they will try to find their way back to their territory. This trip back might include road crossings, where they are at the mercy of cars and trucks. Left alone, box turtles can live for decades. In many states, including Pennsylvania, it is illegal to possess a box turtle taken from the wild.

During the heat of summer, box turtles seek refuge beneath the leaf litter in the woods or along the edges of a marsh or stream. When there is a major spell of hot and dry weather, they enter a state of torpor, known as estivation. As temperatures moderate in late summer and early fall, their activity increases. In preparation for winter's frosty temperatures, box turtles dig a burrow which may be up to two feet deep in the mud, soil, stream bottom, or stump of a fallen tree. The burrow is referred to as a hibernaculum and can be shared by one or two turtles. Their period of dormancy, called brumation, resembles a state of suspended animation. It is characterized by a slowing of the turtle's metabolism, which protects its internal organs even though they can withstand icing for short periods of time.

A friend of mine discovered a significant population of box turtles in his wooded backyard and adjacent land, including some township-owned woods. For several years, he has closely observed these turtles and can now recognize individuals. He has worked with his township supervisors to put up signs designating a protected wildlife area, where building trails and collecting animals is forbidden. A few years ago, I joined his volunteer group to help install silt fencing along a length of highway curbing. Our hope was to block turtles from crossing into busy traffic where they could be crushed by the wheels of a car.

Community science groups, like the Box Turtle Connection in North Carolina, involve dozens of volunteers to gather information about box turtles. Working with biologists, they track the movements of these turtles with radio transmitters attached to their shells. Using a three-pronged antenna and attached receiver, they can locate the turtle's current position and track their movements. The data gleaned from these studies helps scientists develop management plans for protecting the species.

My students and I will never forget the box turtle that interrupted our insect foray. For a moment, I considered picking up the turtle and taking it back to the classroom so that I could show it to some of my other classes. In the end, I decided it was best to leave the turtle alone, reinforcing the message that turtles are best left in their natural habitat. This chance encounter between eighteen second graders and a box turtle remains a highlight of my teaching career. There would be plenty of other opportunities to look for insects. This was a rare, teachable moment.

Say a Little Prayer

I had a surprise companion on my walk. It was a sun-kissed September morning and I was leading a group of students through tall meadow grasses scattered with wildflowers. We were frequently side-tracked by numerous discoveries in what seemed, from a distance, like a still, quiet field. Every few yards demanded an abrupt halt. "What's this?" Forward momentum abandoned, we needed to investigate the striped caterpillar, or the tiny broken bones of a small mammal, or the scattered nest of a bird. This group of young explorers found more in that field than I had when I walked it alone. Midway along the trail, a praying mantid landed on my cap. Immediately, a few eagle-eyed followers spotted it. Pandemonium broke out! They were both terrified and thrilled. I bent lower so that everyone could see it easily. From that point on, the mantid remained with us, riding on my cap, until the trail's end. Wishing it a good day, the students and I transferred our insect friend from cap to field. It had been a memorable morning.

The triangular-shaped head and large bulging eyes of mantids are captivating. Its long, angled thorax and head measure close to half its body length. Suspended in front of its body is a pair of legs bent at the ends. Assuming what might be described as a prayerful position, we afford them a peaceful demeanor. That is until we witness the speed and agility of an ambush. The front legs lined with sharp spikes skewer its prey and keep it in position while being consumed.

Worldwide, there are 1,800 species of mantids. Most of these are inhabitants of the tropics. In the United States there are seventeen species. Three species of mantid are found in our area and two of them, the European mantid (*Mantis religiosa*) and the Chinese mantid (*Tenodera sinensis*) are non-native. The European mantid was first brought into this country from southern Europe in 1899 on nursery stock. It was later sold as a biological control for pests in the garden. During the gypsy moth infestation in the 1980s, European mantids were employed, although with questionable effectiveness, to prey on the moths. Measuring approximately 4" in length, this mantid is greener than the others and sports a bull's-eye pattern under its forelegs. The Chinese mantid can measure up to 5" in length making it the largest of the three. In 1896, the first Chinese mantids showed up at a nursery in the Mt. Airy section of Philadelphia, Pennsylvania and are now found in almost every state and province in North America. Chinese mantid egg cases have been sold to gardeners and farmers for years as a deterrent for insect pests. Unfortunately, the mantids do not discriminate and will eat many beneficial insects including bees and other important pollinator species in the bargain. The Carolina mantid (*Stagmomantis Carolina*) is the smallest mantid at 3" in length. It is rarely seen. While its small size might make it more difficult to find, it also receives robust competition from European and Chinese mantids for both food and territory.

Mantids feed primarily on insects and spiders and will also eat small frogs and lizards. The larger Chinese mantid will even make a meal out of small birds. A lean, green hunting machine, the mantid is well adapted for catching prey. The long neck, or elongated thorax, enables a mantid to swivel its head 180 degrees, a full half circle. It is the only insect that can turn its head from side to side and look back over its shoulder to find prey. It does not have to actively pursue its food. Waiting patiently and ever so still, the mantid scans the area, locates potential prey and once within reach shoots out its long legs for a successful capture.

Praying mantids have five eyes, just like bees, wasps, grasshoppers, and dragonflies. The two large compound eyes provide depth perception and assist in detecting movement. Like humans and other primates, each compound eye has a fovea, a concentrated area of photoreceptor cells that enables the mantid to track and focus unlike many other animals.

Three smaller eyes can be found in the middle of the head for detecting light.

Mantids have exceptional hearing and can pick up frequencies higher than the upper audible level for humans. A single ear, located inside a narrow groove between the legs known as the ventral midline, provides sensitive ultrasonic hearing. They can hear at a range of 30-60 kilohertz, while we max out at 20 kilohertz. They can detect the sounds of bats and will dive to the ground in a series of loops and spirals if approached. Conversely, the human voice is too low for them to hear.

The two antennae on the top its head are used for smell and navigation. They enable the insect to search for food when it tilts its head from side to side. Praying mantids can regenerate a lost antennae, mid-leg, or hind-leg when young. It may take at least one molt to regrow a new appendage and that one appendage may not have the complexity of the original. At times, this process goes awry, and a leg may appear where an antenna was lost.

Several species of mantids employ camouflage to blend in with their natural surroundings and surprise their prey. Each time it molts, or sheds its outgrown exoskeleton, a praying mantid can switch from sporting a dark brown to a green color or vice versa. This enables it to blend best with the bark or green leaves of its current surroundings. Some species of mantids develop more vibrant colors, like the pink orchid mantid found in southeast Asia. Temperature, humidity, and light intensity are all important factors in determining color at a given moment.

In September and October, before the first frost, the female prepares for winter by depositing a cluster of eggs covered with a thin veneer of silk. The eggs are surrounded by a frothy foam, resembling toothpaste, which hardens to form a casing like brown styrofoam. Each egg case, known as an ootheca, contains between two and three hundred eggs. Although usually fastened to twigs and stems, I have seen egg cases attached to buildings, fences, and chairs. When the weather gets warmer and we move through the spring months, the young emerge to resemble miniature adults. Born with voracious appetites, you can release them into your garden, where they will immediately begin eating any insects they might find. Should food items be unavailable, they will not hesitate to eat each other. While mantid egg cases are fascinating to observe and inspect, they should never be kept for any period indoors. They will hatch in four to six weeks in the warmth of your home, filling it with an invasion of hundreds. If you were able to scoop them all up at once, and I don't think that has ever been successfully accomplished, they would not survive a release into the winter's cold temperatures.

The flightless female Carolina mantid, three inches in length, outsizes the male. Common in the southern states, the Carolina mantid has expanded its range as far north as New York and Connecticut with possible further expansion. A Carolina mantid's egg case is flattened and elongated with cream and brown stripes along the top. While the size and shape differentiate it from the cube-shaped Chinese mantis egg case, it also looks like it is made of styrofoam.

During mating season, the smaller male mantid, is sometimes referred to as the "headless lover." He is lucky if he survives the day. When ready to mate, he approaches her with utmost care, usually from behind after she has captured an insect. Should she see him, she will snatch him, like any other insect, to cannibalize. Beginning with his eyes the female will continue with the rest of his head. Remarkably, the headless corpse can continue to consummate the relationship. The French naturalist and entomologist, Jean Henri Fabré, wrote these words, "I have seen it done with my own eyes and have not recovered from my astonishment."

During the early weeks of September, I can almost guarantee my students and I will find praying mantids during our outdoor excursions. They are living among the leaves or clinging to stalks of grass in the school's wet meadow. I encourage students to search for them and when found to observe with eyes only.

Heading out later that day with a new group of eager explorers I hear it, "Look what I found!" Perfect! Another great discovery!

Percussion Virtuosos

It never fails to amaze me. Specific sounds accompany each season. Like a piece of well-crafted music, there are choruses whose volume builds to a crescendo, then resolves to introduce a seasonal soloist. Beginning in late March, spring peepers, toads, woodcocks, and whip-poor-wills perform for our spring concert series. As summer transitions to fall, the percussive sound of insects gives rise to a completely different musical genre. Grasshoppers and cicadas dominate the day and crickets and katydids fill the nocturnal soundscape. On an August night, I am compelled to head outside to savor their call and response rhythms. These virtuosos speak to me of life energized and ever present.

These six-legged musicians have been playing together for a long time. In fact, over two hundred million years ago, the insect world was performing its cacophonous concert of buzzes, clicks, chirps, and trills. These were some of the first animal sounds made on our planet. Long before the advent of Homo sapiens, the sounds of insects increased in volume and intensity with the approaching autumn.

Unlike mammals who produce sound by passing air through vocal cords in their throats, insects produce sound using parts of their bodies. Male katydids and crickets have a file and scraper arrangement on their front

wings. Rubbing their forewings together generates vibrations much like a bow on a fiddle string. Grasshoppers rub one of their hind legs against one of their hard forewings, causing the wing to vibrate. Cicadas have drum-like organs on the sides of their bodies, which snap in and out. Most of the sounds that we hear are produced by males, so it is theorized that these are mating calls. However, cicadas continue to be heard long after mating occurs.

The symphonic sounds of insects resemble those found in the percussion section of an orchestra. A percussionist pays close attention to the dynamics on a page of music. The markings of dynamics indicate how soft or loud a passage should sound. In much the same way, although without printed music, insects respond to the rise and fall of temperature. They produce a varied tempo while maintaining a vibrant pulsing beat. High-pitched notes are emitted to carry long distances through the night. While it has been said that insects "sing" in the key of C sharp, I believe there is a lot more variety. Sitting on my deck any night in August and September, I am immersed in 360-degrees of varying buzzes, calls, clicks, and scrapes. Settling back to enjoy all that these musical virtuosos have to offer, I find myself comparing their sounds to those I hear in a concert hall. Out here though, the musicians are unconcerned with the rigidities of conductors and compositions. If there was a written score, the entire piece would be marked "fortissimo" as the music this evening is almost deafening. Their sole goal is to sound loud enough and long enough to attract a mate.

One of my favorite nighttime sounds belongs to the katydid. Well camouflaged during the day, with shiny green oval wings resembling leaves, they move about silently. The cover of night seems to lend them another persona. As I listen, I imagine that the katydids are hanging out in the trees arguing amongst themselves. When they rub their forewings twice together, it sounds as if they say the word "Katy." Rubbing them three times produces the sound of "Katy did." When they rub them four times together, I imagine them saying, "Katy didn't." According to legend, "Katy" was a young woman accused of murder. To this day the katydids continue to argue about whether she did or did not commit the crime.

The most familiar of our insect musicians are the field crickets. Shiny black with long antennae, they live in fields, marshes, and backyards. As the males scrape their wings together, they produce a high-pitched chirp. It is very pleasing to our ears and, I assume, to the female crickets. Known as "stridulation," the faster they move their wings, the higher the pitch. Another cricket, the snowy tree cricket, can provide us with the approximate temperature. If you count the number of chirps in fifteen seconds and add forty, you will have a rough estimate of the temperature in degrees Fahrenheit. For example, if the cricket sings 20 times within 15 seconds, the temperature is sixty degrees Fahrenheit. Male and female crickets detect sound with a pair of tympanal organs on their legs which vibrate in response to moving air molecules. Female crickets do not produce sound. They respond to the male's call through a behavior known as "phonotaxis," or moving toward the sound by walking or flying.

Grasshoppers produce their strident music by running their hind legs against their forewings. When the pegs on the inside of its leg contact the thickened edge of the wings, it works in much the same way as a bow on a stringed instrument. Unlike crickets, grasshoppers detect sound through organs located in the abdomen. While they do most of their singing during daylight hours, it is not unusual to hear them in the evening.

Cicadas are stout-bodied insects with big eyes and long angular wings. Most of their lives are spent deep in the ground as nymphs, feeding on tree roots. When they emerge, they are still nymphs until they molt for the final time. Once they split their shells, or exoskeletons, emerging as a flying insect, they move up into the trees. Cicadas sing, mate, lay their eggs, and die all in the span of a few weeks. Each summer, there are annual hatchings which stir the imagination of any young child who finds an abandoned shell. During years when the 17-year cicadas appear, we find ourselves overwhelmed by a cacophony of sound and surprise guests at our outdoor events.

There are a variety of species, including periodical cicadas, annual cicadas, and dog-day harvest flies. All cicadas have prominent eyes set wide apart, short antennae, and membranous front legs. Both sexes have membranous structures, called "tympana," to detect sounds. Most species appear every year, while the periodical cicadas emerge every seventeen years. The eyes of the periodical cicadas are bright red, while other species have green, black, or brown eyes.

Male cicadas produce a throbbing sound using drum-like organs along their abdomens. As they snap these drums in and out, they make a loud vibrating sound that sends shivers up the spine. They do most of their singing during the daylight hours, but there are usually a few that persist into the night. Louder than a Rolling Stones concert, the sound of thousands buzzing at the same time can be deafening. And much like a Stones concert, there is potential for humans to suffer hearing loss if they have been in close range for too long.

With windows wide open, I hear the night sounds loud and clear. They connect me to the vibrant lives of musicians not of my own species. As the weather gets colder, I know their music will gradually fade. The katydids will give up their age-old argument, the energetic fiddle tunes of crickets and grasshoppers will slow to a dirge, and the cicadas will drum to the slowest setting on the metronome. Beginning in November, their concert series will be "Closed for the Season." I, for one, will be looking forward to their return engagement.

Champions of the Wind

I could feel it in my bones. Gone is the hot, humid air of summer, swept away by the northwest winds. Multicolored leaves spiral into the air, yellowing field grasses bend in the breeze, and wildflowers release seed parachutes to reach destinations unknown. I have been waiting and watching for this day. It is the type that heralds summer's transition and the coming of thousands. Migration is on; the hawks are coming.

My home in southeastern Pennsylvania lies in an epicenter of hawk watching. An hour and fifteen minutes north and west, Hawk Mountain straddles the Kittatinny Ridge of the Appalachian Mountains. Winds deflected off the mountain ridge create an updraft on which the hawks gain altitude. Spiraling columns of warmed air rise from the adjacent valleys forming thermals. Migrating birds use these updrafts and thermals to preserve precious energy stores on their way south. Upon entering a thermal, they soar in spiral formation to ever increasing heights. When they reach the top, the hawks stream out of the column at great speeds towards the next. Due to a combination of geology, geography, and wind patterns, the Kittatinny Ridge is a perfect migratory flyway. During the early years of the twentieth century, these factors, among others, worked against the raptors. Some people viewed the hawks as menaces to their livestock. Others were simply shooting them for sport. Rosalie Edge, a prominent conservationist disturbed by the senseless slaughter, purchased the property in 1934 which became the Hawk Mountain Sanctuary. Aided by numerous like-minded individuals, they stopped the hunting and began the arduous task of transforming this area into a premier spot for protecting and observing birds of prey. For over thirty years, I've visited Hawk Mountain on a regular basis. There were days when I sat at North Lookout for hours without seeing a single raptor, while on other days a continuous stream of hawks soared overhead throughout the day. Most of the time, the birds appear as specks in the distance. However, on a trip with my students, we were able to witness a golden eagle fly only feet above our heads.

Travelling south and east, two and a half hours away, Cape May Point State Park in New Jersey proclaims its location as the "raptor capitol of North America." When the weather is right, there are days with astounding numbers of raptors, shorebirds, and other migrants. Bordered on its western shores by the Delaware Bay and the Atlantic Ocean on the east, migrating hawks naturally funnel towards the Cape May peninsula. Here they stop and feed in the wet meadows, woods, and ponds, replenishing energy spent on their long flights. Before continuing their arduous journeys south, they eat to enlarge their fat stores needed to ensure successful flights to their destinations. I've been fortunate to view some of these birds in the process of capturing their prey. As I walked through the maritime forest trail, a peregrine falcon flew overhead with a pigeon in its talons. Later, standing on a platform, I watched an osprey dive for fish in the pond, making huge splashes upon impact.

On late summer days when the temperature drops and the winds pick up, I head over to Fort Washington State Park, about half an hour away. This is the home of the Militia Hill Hawk Watch. Around the middle of September, on the cusp of fall, the broad-winged hawks move through. If I am lucky enough to be there on a day when the birds are moving through, gratitude washes over me. How fortunate I am to be in the right place at the right time.

Key to planning a successful hawk-watching trip is factoring in the weather forecast. Following a few disappointing forays, I came to realize that it doesn't help to schedule a trip more than a few days in advance. I have found that humid days produce the least activity. Perhaps the birds, like myself, feel a bit grounded on days of oppressive heat. Strong northwest winds provide lift and direction for these birds. These same winds move me to grab my binoculars and head out to witness their journey south.

Hawk watching season runs from early September through most of November, with optimal times for each of the species that regularly pass through our area. At times, experienced birders note individuals not normally found along the flyway. These are accidental species which may have been blown off course in an earlier storm. Migrating monarch butterflies and green darner dragonflies are an added bonus to a hawk watcher's day.

When watching birds in woods, fields, and wetlands, birders look for characteristic field marks. Observing raptors from a distance, these markings are hard to see. It's best to look for a general impression based on size, shape, flight pattern, and behavior. Soaring hawks, known as buteos, have broad wings and rounded tails. They are frequently found in open fields and along highways, where they can survey a wide swath of land in search of small mammals. The smaller, leaner accipiters feed primarily on other bird species. Their flight resembles the opening stanza of Beethoven's fifth symphony (flap, flap, flap, glide…). They have long narrow tails and short rounded wings, perfect for navigating through trees to catch prey in wooded areas. Falcons have streamlined bodies and pointed wings, making them the fastest birds of prey. In addition, there are four other categories of diurnal raptors in the northeast, represented by vultures, harriers, eagles, and osprey.

For sheer number of birds, I have found the middle of September to be the best time to go hawk watching. Every year, the broad-winged hawks open the season, whirling and spiraling overhead, like objects in a boiling cauldron, giving rise to the term, a "kettle" of hawks. Gliding on these currents of warm air affords the birds the opportunity to preserve precious energy. On a good day, they seem able to glide from the top of one thermal to the next without a single wingbeat. Approximately the size of a crow, the broad-winged hawk is a small stocky hawk with a series of black and white bands on its rounded tail. Every year, there are one or two days that mark the pinnacle of its migration. I had gone hawk watching for many years before finally experiencing a "big day" on September 15, 2013. Over fifteen thousand broad-winged hawks flew past the Militia Hill Hawk Watch on that one day. A decade later, over five thousands hawks were seen. While there are sixteen species of raptors that pass through my local hawk watch area, the sheer numbers of broad-winged hawks surpass all the rest.

Stationed at the hawk watch, from September through November, volunteers do their best to count the number of hawks passing through. This requires considerable skill because the hawks often appear as dots in the distance. Generally, there are several counters, and amazingly, they seem to end up with the same number, or something close. I asked one of the counters how he counts the hawks when there are hundreds in the sky at once. His answer spoke to years of experience as he relayed the variety of factors he must consider. Slowly scanning the skies with binoculars that offer a wide field of view, he moves from one image to another in the direction the birds are coming from. In some instances, the counters focus on a section of a kettle and extrapolate the rest. In other cases, the counters will wait until the birds are moving from one thermal to the next before they count them. The birds can only get so high within a thermal before they stream out of it and head to the bottom of the next one.

Birds of the forest interior, broad-winged hawks breed in every state east of the Rockies and a large swath of eastern Canada. For most of the year, they are seldom seen, preferring a solitary existence. During nesting season, the adults stay together with their young. More frequently heard than seen, the call is a high-pitched plaintive whistle lasting two to four seconds. Generally, there is a short first note followed by a longer second note. Singing an octave higher than his female counterpart, distinguishes male from female.

Come fall, the broad-wings leave their northern homes to winter in Central and South America. Once private and elusive, these birds come together, joining hundreds, even thousands of its kind to form giant kettles in the sky. Reluctant to fly over open water, they prefer a land route where rising thermals and mountain updrafts enable them to travel extensive distances with minimal effort. Using radio transmitters, scientists tracked four broad-winged hawks flying an average of 4,350 miles from Canada to northern South America, travelling sixty-nine miles each day and resting at night.

On the heels of broad-wing migration, late September and October skies are dominated by sharp-shinned and Cooper's hawks. Osprey and bald eagles might be seen any time in the early fall, while the best time to spot a golden eagle is in mid-November, near the close of the season. In Veracruz, Mexico, birds of prey concentrate in such great numbers in the fall that people call it a "river of raptors."

Our attitude towards hawks has changed dramatically over the past hundred years. Once considered pests, they were frequently shot, with bounties offered for the dead birds. Today, they are protected by the Migratory Bird Treaty Act and over two hundred hawk watch stations in North America monitor daily sightings. Powered by thermals and bolstered by the wind, migrating hawks present one of the finest spectacles in nature. In the final days of summer, the broad-winged hawks offer a prelude to autumn, reminding us that change is in the wind.

Appendix

The Making of a Community Scientist

by Ron Smith

On summer evenings as a child, I made sure I took advantage of the long hours of daylight. Finishing dinner quickly, I returned outside to resume whatever activity or exploration had been interrupted. Every minute offered the possibility of discovery or adventure. I'm not sure whether it's because my siblings and I spent so much time outside or if it was because I was born with a thirst to know more about it, but outdoors became the place I always wanted to be.

Our frequent explorations of natural places led us to know which plants would be blooming at various times during the season. Likewise, we became familiar with the movements and behavior of animals within these same habitats. Though I don't remember ever verifying it, our focused attention enabled us to approximate both the time of day and season based on the plants in bloom and animal activity. From the arrival of warblers in the forests to the flowering of a sundew plant to the breeding of carpenter frogs, we were learning nature's timing.

Perhaps no species brought together the clock and calendar like fireflies. During June and July evenings our backyard came alive with the magical glow of these bioluminescent invertebrates. For us, the flashes of these insects brought comfort as dark descended outside. Delighted, we sought to identify the patches of garden where the most fireflies could be found. In the garden shed we kept our sampling equipment: nets, guides, and containers for holding specimens. We would catch the lightning bugs (insects which are actually beetles) and examine them closely in mason jars with holes punched in the lids. We kept samples of vegetation in the jars for the fireflies to perch on while we observed them and were sure to let them go after our brief close encounter. We were absolutely mesmerized by their biology, and we were inspired to draw them, write about them and attempt photos of their intermittent flashes, sure that one of the images would be worthy of a National Geographic Magazine cover.

Like many of the other creatures we were fortunate enough to interact with, we took for granted their presence in our garden. We assumed they were permanent spring and summer residents in our backyard community. My early years of exploration gave way to a more formal study of biology when I went to college in New England. Away for extended periods of time, I was not around to observe the effects of development—more houses, more roads, transformation of the natural vegetation to more ornamental species and the use of pesticides that went along with the disruption and replacement of plant communities. I didn't realize at first that the dark of evening had been replaced by the use of streetlights, ornamental landscape lights and the floodlights used on back porches. All of which has forever altered the nightscape for insects dependent on communication through tiny flashes of cold light.

Professional and community scientists monitor species that are known to be a measure of the health of habitats and ecosystems. These creatures are referred to as indicator species. Fireflies certainly fit the bill. Easy to spot and loved by even the most ardent entomophobe, fireflies can serve as an invertebrate ambassador. Healthy habitat for fireflies likely means healthy habitat for other insect species.

Over the last two decades my work in science education has evolved to focus on the significant benefits of community science. Projects that collect data and provide information about the health of populations and habitats can be very useful to the professional conservation community. Expanding on established projects that monitor fireflies, we have carried out backyard inventories in two towns involving several families. We have worked to compile a database of firefly activity and relative abundance in the gardens of our homes. Due to their wide geographical distribution, adaptability to habitat diversity and a biology that makes them easy to document, fireflies can be a great starting point for any community science effort.

Many of the creatures Craig Newberger describes in the pages of this book are found near our homes, schools and communities. Access to nature is something that we should hold dear. All of us are called to be naturalists and stewards of the biodiversity found in nature. It is part of our own biology to be curious about the environment in which we live.

Today every species needs protection, surely some more than others, and we can be participants in this effort. Simple acts and observations can spark a community effort towards learning more about the natural world while becoming actively engaged in contributing to the knowledge, wonder and protection of nature. If you are reading this book, you are needed for these efforts! So let's get started.... Together!

Acknowledgments

It would be impossible to list all the family, friends, teachers, students, and colleagues that have played a part in this book. My life has been enriched in so many ways by the people that have shared time with me outdoors.

Special thanks to my wife and best friend, Trudy Phillips, who has worked with me every step along the way. Her mastery of language and her skills in editing and proofreading were invaluable throughout this project.

I extend a shout-out to Ted Gilman, Pete Salmansohn, Mercedes Villamil, Ret Turner, Tom Tyning, and Steve Mason for reviewing these essays and offering feedback to ensure accuracy and clarity. I am tremendously grateful for their interpretive skills and insights.

Once again, it was a pleasure to work with Ed Flickinger, publisher of Grackle Books on this second volume of essays. His support and guidance continue to provide me a pathway to share my excitement and respect for the natural world.

Biographies

Craig Newberger

Author Craig Newberger served as the Lower School science coordinator at Germantown Academy in Pennsylvania over three decades. Combining hands-on investigations with outdoor explorations, Craig nurtured a passion for science and nature in thousands of inquisitive minds. He led a variety of natural science trips for his students and their families, ranging from Costa Rica to Cape Cod. Craig's belief in immersing students in firsthand experiences led him to dedicate decades of summers in Maine where he and his wife, Trudy, directed the National Audubon Society Youth Ecology Camp on Hog Island, founded and directed the Family Camp, and joined the instructional team for Audubon's camp for educators. Craig has also worked as a naturalist at the Cape Cod Museum of Natural History and directed an environmental education program connected with the Cape Cod National Seashore. Craig plays guitar and hammered dulcimer and he is known for his sing-alongs at assemblies and campfires. Craig is the author of *Spring Processional: Encounters with a Waking World.*

Steve Morello

Steve Morello is an award-winning photographer, writer, and storyteller, known for telling a story with his images. Steve created the Little River Photo Workshops to share his skill and craft with others on his property in North Berwick, Maine. Steve is a National Geographic certified photo instructor and teaches for National Geographic and Lindblad Expeditions on expeditions around the planet. He is the author of *The Travelling Nature Photographer.*

Sherrie York

A self-taught printmaker and compulsive wanderer of landscapes, Sherrie York finds her inspiration in the natural world. A long-ago college field trip to draw backyard chickens was the genesis of a career that has encompassed environmental education, natural history illustration, and fine art. Her illustration clients have included several national and international conservation organizations and her fine art is included in corporate, private, and museum collections worldwide.

Ron Smith

Ron Smith established the environmental science and education program in the Haddonfield School district where he currently teaches. Along with faculty and staff from the Academy of Natural Sciences of Drexel University, Ron leads community science projects along the coast of New Jersey with focus on shorebirds and horseshoe crabs. He directs the Drexel University Environmental Science Leadership Academy and founded the Life Science Field Training Institute for Pinelands Preservation Alliance, a program that trains educators in field methods in community science. Ron is the author of *Adventures in Community Science*.

liance

0 1 9 6 *